THE CLASSICS
OF **WESTERN**
SPIRITUALITY

THE CLASSICS OF WESTERN SPIRITUALITY
A Library of the Great Spiritual Masters

Nil Sorsky
THE COMPLETE WRITINGS

EDITED AND TRANSLATED BY
GEORGE A. MALONEY, S.J.

PREFACE BY
JOHN L. MINA

PAULIST PRESS
NEW YORK • MAHWAH, N.J.

Cover art by Sister Mary Grace Thul, O.P.

Book design by Theresa M. Sparacio

Cover and caseside design by A. Michael Velthaus

Library of Congress Cataloging-in-Publication Data

Nil, Sorskiæi, Saint, ca. 1433–1508.
   [Works. English. 2003]
   The writings of Nil Sorsky / edited and translated by George A. Maloney.
     p. cm.
   Includes bibliographical references and index.
   ISBN 0-8091-3810-7; ISBN 0-8091-0497-0
   1. Spiritual life—Russkaëïia pravoslavnaëïia ëtiserkov§. 2. Monasticism and religious orders, Orthodox Eastern—Russia—Rules. 3. Nil, Sorskiæi, Saint, ca. 1433–1508—Correspondence. I. Maloney, George A., 1924– II. Title.
   BX597.N52 A2 2003
   248.4′819—dc21

                                                              2002153156

Published by Paulist Press
997 Macarthur Boulevard
Mahwah, New Jersey 07430

www.paulistpress.com

Printed and bound in the
United States of America

Table of Contents

Editor of This Volume

GEORGE A. MALONEY, S.J., was ordained in Rome as a priest of the Russian Byzantine Rite in 1957. He earned a doctorate in Eastern Christian Theology in 1962, summa cum laude, from the Pontifical Oriental Institute.

Father Maloney served as founder and editor of an ecumenical journal, *Diakonia*, for seventeen years to promote dialogue between Orthodox and Roman Catholics. He is the author of sixty-three books, including his editing and translation of the Paulist volume in 1992 of the writings of Pseudo-Macarius.

He taught theology at Fordham University for sixteen years and was founder and director of the John XXIII Institute for Eastern Christian Studies at Fordham University until 1984. Fr. Maloney has established himself as an outstanding author of works on prayer and Eastern Christian spirituality as applied to the daily life of Western Christians. He now directs Contemplative Ministries in Seal Beach, California.

Author of the Preface

REV. JOHN L. MINA, archivist of the Ruthenian Byzantine Catholic Archdiocese of Pittsburgh and ecumenical representative to the theological committee of the Christian Associates of Southwest Pennsylvania, was born in Nancy, France. His parents were political refugees from Czechoslovakia. He completed a B.A. (with highest honors) in Russian at the University of California, Santa Barbara, in 1972. In 1974, he earned an M.A. in Slavic Languages and Literatures and in 1979, a Ph.D. at the University of California, Berkeley. The subject of his dissertation, which he researched at the Academy of Sciences Institute of Russian Literature in Saint Petersburg, was the Russian religious oral epic. Rev. Mina pursued theological and historical studies at the Pontifical Gregorian University and Oriental Institute in Rome. He taught at the Centre d'Etudes Russes at Meudon, France, University of Kentucky at Lexington and Saints Cyril and Methodius Seminary in Pittsburgh. He is the author of articles about Russian literature and spiritual history. His monograph on the history of the Ruthenian Church was published by the Catholic Historical Society of Western Pennsylvania.

to Dr. John Mooney,
a Modern Disciple
of St. Nil Sorsky

Preface

The writings of the great fifteenth-century Russian spiritual master Nil Sorsky form a high peak in a tragic but also verdant and seminal period in the history of Byzantine Christendom. The tragedy first struck in 1204, when the rerouted Fourth Crusade captured the queen of cities and heart of the Byzantine spiritual commonwealth, Constantinople. A second blow came in 1237, with the eruption of Asiatic nomads, welded together by the cruel genius of Ghengiz Khan into an irresistible force, and led into Europe by Batu Khan, founder of the Golden Horde. Within five years the proud but disunited princely towns of ancient *Rus'* lay smoldering, their populations slain or dispersed or led into captivity. Hearing of the death of the Great Khan in Mongolia, Batu Khan rounded off his campaign with a *razzia* through the recently reemerged Orthodox states of the Balkans.

Battered from both West and East "for their sins," as contemporary Russian chroniclers and the great orator of the thirteenth century Serapion of Vladimir explained it, Byzantine Christians still found within themselves the creative impulses to initiate a spiritual, artistic, and even political revival, at the forefront of which, along with some remarkable rulers, stood farsighted patriarchs, metropolitans, and learned monks.

The inspiration for this renewal, as well as the religious and cultural will to resist the intruders, came, in great part, from a spiritual-ascetic movement known as *hesychasm*. This tradition has remained largely alien to the Christian West, though it is founded on venerable patristic writings and praxis, including, among others, the traditions of the Cappadocian and Syrian fathers, John Climacus,

1

and the author of what are known as the "Pseudo-Macarian" texts. Hesychast ideas, which had a steady development in Byzantine mysticism, were reinvigorated at the end of the thirteenth century in the Athonite monasteries by the arrival of Gregory of Sinai, and in the early fourteenth century, they were ably defended against determined challengers, foreign and domestic, by the great Gregory Palamas. A disciple of Gregory of Sinai, Theodosius of Tyrnovo brought this tradition to the northern Balkans, while other disciples such as Kallistos and Philotheos disseminated it from the patriarchal throne of Constantinople. This movement crossed ethnic and political boundaries. It revitalized literature and literary languages, sacred art and architecture. In a short time it produced a truly encyclopedic effort to reedit, translate, and systematize the entire heritage of Eastern spiritual writings. Exponents of hesychast art and letters moved freely from one part of the Byzantine common-wealth to another, finding in each new country employment and like-minded companions. In Russia of the fourteenth and fifteenth centuries, alongside the native Russian hesychasts—the astute and powerful Metropolitan Alexis of Moscow, the restorer of Russia's soul and initiator of the peaceful colonization of the North, Abbot Sergius of Radonezh, the great missionary bishop and linguist Stephen of Perm, the hagiographer Epiphanius the Wise, and the sublime iconographer Andrei Rublev—there appear the erudite and long-suffering Bulgarian-born Metropolitan Cyprian, the inspiring iconographer and initiator of a new dynamic style Theophanes the Greek, and the great hagiographer Pachomius the Serb.

At the basis of hesychasm there lay an intense belief in the nearness of the sacred, a *mystical realism* that stressed the ineffable, all-upholding, and transforming self-manifestation of God, who is Love, and who pours forth his divine, life-creating energies on all through his Holy Spirit. Those who rightly seek him become com-pletely filled with the uncreated light that shone forth from Christ at his Transfiguration on Mount Tabor. This light is a sign and result of *theosis* or deification: the becoming ever more perfectly in the image and likeness of the Heavenly Father. To attain this, that is, to refurbish the divine mirror in himself, man must undertake an arduous journey of self-knowledge and self-mastery, overcome his passions, and become whole again. This process is rooted not in man's willfulness, but in growing ever nearer to Christ, who conquered sin and death by uniting Divinity to humanity, divine will with human will, in perfect and complete symphony. Stillness (*hesychia*), inner beauty, and a quiet joy are the fruits of constantly turning one's mind inward, communing in one's innermost heart with the Savior through the continuous, purifying repetition of the divine Name, and accruing ever more his Holy Spirit. The hesychast, however, is not an escapist, even if he must withdraw for a while into solitude in order to find himself. The true hesychast, through his prayer, consolation, work, and art, radiates inner stillness, beauty, and joy throughout a vain and disordered world. His work is always one of restoration, not rejection. Thus the great insight of Byzantine theology, going back to Maximus the Confessor, that nature presupposes grace and beauty manifests God is brought to full realization in the profoundly personal, but never atomistic, hesychast religious praxis. It produces an intensely religious world view. This is very different from the sterner Western view of autonomous, albeit depraved, nature always opposing grace, a view that helped open the way to extreme nominalism and eventually to the secularism of the Renaissance.

Secularism also had its proponents in Byzantium. These generally took their inspiration from Classical Hellenic philosophy. Pride in their Greek heritage became especially pronounced in some circles as a reaction to the humiliation of the "Latin" Crusader occupation. The demands of an all-embracing religious world view were far less palatable to this crowd than those of a largely formalistic Church pushed into an intellectual corner. As a result, they vehemently opposed the hesychasts until the "Palamite" councils of 1347 and 1351 forced them to tone down their vehemence.

In *Rus'*, secularist-rationalist currents first burst forth in Novgorod, the great trading republic of the north, which was open to both Western and Eastern influences. In the late fourteenth century a group called, for reasons that are not completely clear, *Strigol'niki* (Barbers) made a brief appearance, belittling the clergy and mocking icons. They passed out of view shortly after an outraged populace hurled some of their leaders into the freezing waters of the Volkhov River. Yet during the next century, following the visit of a certain "prince of Taman," Zachariah, in the retinue of Prince Michael of Kiev, a vassal of the Polish-Lithuanian state sent to Novgorod to bolster the anti-Muscovite party, there appeared a group called the *Zhidovstvuiushchie* (Judaizers). These generally maintained a cautious reticence before outsiders about their true beliefs. Their numbers included some members of the married clergy as well as some educated laymen.

Archbishop Gennadius of Novgorod sounded the alarm around 1489, when he turned for help to several distinguished clerics, including the learned hesychast starets (elder) Nil Sorsky and the renowned abbot Joseph Volotsky. The situation was all the more critical for the Russian Church because among the supporters of the Judaizers was Princess Helen, the mother of the heir apparent Dmitry and daughter of Prince Stephen of Moldavia. Also in their number were Theodore Kuritsyn, who was Ivan III the Great's chancellor, and Metropolitan Zosima of Moscow. The intrigues that followed have been subjected to differing and very biased interpretations by contemporaries of the events as well as by later researchers. It is important not to confuse the attitudes and actions of Nil Sorsky and Joseph Volotsky, both of whom were canonized by the Russian Church, with the later accounts and polemics of such followers as the ambitious Vassian Patrikeev, whose father was first cousin of Grand Prince Ivan III, and the wily Metropolitan Daniel. Both Nil Sorsky and Joseph Volotsky were adamant in their defense of Christianity. Nil Sorsky also partially contributed to the creation and dissemination of Joseph Volotsky's work "Enlightener—Account About the Newly Appeared Heresy" on the eve of the Council of 1504, which helped lead to the condemnation of the heretics by that council.

The long hiatus between the discovery of the heretics and their final defeat was due undoubtedly to their high protectors and the latter's influence over the Grand Prince. For his efforts to expose the heretics, Archbishop Gennadius was punished in 1499 by the confiscation of many Church and monastic lands in Novgorod and, eventually, by dismissal from his post. Chancellor Kuritsyn used this precedent to set in motion a larger plan, to which the Grand Prince was not altogether unsympathetic, to divest the Church, particularly the monasteries, of their lands and thus fatally weaken the Church. The secularization issue, in fact, was raised at a council in 1503, which was attended by both Nil and Joseph. The *Slovo Inoe* (One Particular Discourse), a work that antedates other accounts of that council by decades but was only recently discovered and was published by J. Begunov in 1964, indicates that the struggle at this council was between Ivan III and the majority of the clergy, not between Joseph and Nil, although the latter, following an old Byzantine tradition, supported the idea of the *nonaccruing* (*nesti-azhanie*) by monasteries of great earthly wealth. According to the *Slovo*, Nil mentioned this ideal in a conversation with the Grand Prince. Still, Nil and the Grand Prince understood this issue on different planes, and it is hardly imaginable that under the prevailing circumstances of the desperate struggle against the heretics, Nil would have tolerated any attack on the Church.

Prescinding from the intrigues that broke out after the death of Nil Sorsky in 1508 and that in no way elucidate the spiritual truths contained in the great elder's writings, we should, in all fairness, stop briefly before the figure of his much-maligned contemporary Joseph Volotsky, who, by the command of Grand-Prince Basil III, was not even permitted to answer the attacks made against him by Vassian Patrikeev. Now if the *Testament* and *Rule* of Nil Sorsky witness to the awesome transfiguring power of the Divine Triune Life encountered in the mystical stillness of the innermost heart, the *Enlightener* of Joseph Volotsky testifies to a mighty incarnational dimension in Russian spirituality. This is especially evident in the section *"Slova ob ikonakh"* ("Discourses about Icons"). For Joseph the icons, so repugnant to the Novgorod rationalists, are more than vehicles through which we rise to contemplation and devotion. They are windows through which the prototypes look into us and become personally present to us. This immediacy and familiarity of the sacred not only shines in the icons, but can permeate the whole of human life. The heavenly becomes inculcated in the earthly and all life is subsumed in piety. As this happens, the Church assumes guidance over every facet of human endeavor, and the state supports the Church's work.

The visions of Nil and Joseph are not incompatible; in fact, they can be complementary. Interestingly, Nil took candidates for his skete only after they had completed training in traditional monasteries. The heights of contemplation and self-mastery presume a grounding in piety and Christian living.

Ultimately, it was not Joseph's vision that extinguished Nil's, but the exigencies of empire and the dawning of the age of secularism, which tolerated only a veneer of religiosity. Fortunately, there is a Gladsome Light that cannot be extinguished, and the present translations are an important help to those who seek that Light.

John L. Mina

Abbreviations

DRB:	*Echos d'Orient* (Paris).
Izd. OLDP:	*Izdanie Obschestva ljubitel' pis'mennosti* (St. Petersburg, 1878–1911).
OC:	*Orientalia Christiana* (Rome: Pontifical Oriental Institute [POI]).
OCA:	*Orientalia Christiana Analecta* (Rome: POI).
OCP:	*Orientalia Christiana Periodica* (Rome: POI).
PDP:	*Pannyatniki drevnei pis'mennosti* (St. Petersburg, 1817–1925).
PRIB. K TVOR:	*Pribavlenija k Tvorenijam Svjatyx Otcev v russkom perevode.*
PG:	*Patrologiae cursus completus: Series Graeca*, ed. Migne (Paris).
PL:	*Patrologiae cursus completus: Series Latina*, ed. Migne (Paris).
Prav. Sob:	*Pravoslavns Sobesednik*
PSRL:	*Polnoe sobranie russkix letopisei*
RH:	*Russian Hesychasm*, George A. Maloney, S.J. (The Hague: Mouton, 1973).
RIB:	*Russkaja istoricheskaja biblioteka.*
ROC:	*Revue d'Orient Chretien* (Paris, 1896 f.f.).
SGGD:	*Sobranie Gosudarstvennyx Gramot.* 5 Tomes (Moscow, 1813–1894).
TODL:	*Trudy Otdela drevnerusskoj literatury*, Adamemii Nauk.
Zeitschr. f. S.:	*Zeitschrift für Slawistik.*

N.B.: I have used the Library of Congress (Washington, D.C.) to translate the Slavonic and modern Russian alphabets to the English alphabet.

Introduction

Today we are witnessing a tremendous upheaval in the country that for seventy-five years under communism was known as the U.S.S.R. Newly discovered freedoms and forms of free democracy never before experienced by the Russian people are being enjoyed by all the citizens of what is now known as the Commonwealth of Unified States. We see great confusion and much suffering on all levels of economic, social, religious, and political life as gigantic measures are being taken to free the Russian people from the yoke of totalitarian dictatorship and yet to teach them free democracy and individual enterprise hitherto unknown to them.

In the history of each nation there occur periods when the former existing order seems to have worn out its usefulness and new times demand radical change. At such times providence provides the leaders to effect such changes. A critical transitional period in the history of the Russian people, comparable to what is today happening, was taking place during the fifteenth and sixteenth centuries. And St. Nil Sorsky would have a quiet, but prophetic role to call the Christians of Russia, then and even now, to a vibrant, deeply interior spiritual life in contrast to the externalism of a form of Christianity that became more and more associated with the wealthy political leaders of the emerging Russian Empire.

FORMATION OF THE ALL-RUSSIAN EMPIRE

Russia's feudal appanages were dissolving and giving way to a united Moscow empire under the first Tsar, Ivan III. He became

"Tsar Ivan, Grand Prince, Autocrat of All-Russia." His duties, after the fall of Constantinople in 1453 to the Turks, were "to care for all souls and all Orthodox Christendom."[1] The seeds of Moscow as Third Rome had been long ago planted and now were bursting forth in full fruit.[2] Backing the Tsar was the group of Moscow metropolitans eager to detach their ecclesiastical jurisdiction from that of Constantinople with Joseph of Volokolamsk (1440–1515) as their leader. He in his dynamic style formulated his theory of submission to the Tsar in these words: "He is the lord of all lords in the whole of Russia. God has given him all power and his name is endowed with all authority. God has placed him on the imperial throne, being of one mind with him in judgment and grace."[3] This political theory of church-and-state relationship determined the whole form he gave to his monastic Rule with its heavy emphasis on gigantic monastic possessions.

Nil's ideal of evangelical poverty and total dedication of his monks to the interior life of contemplation and austere asceticism of solitude and control of one's thoughts would clash with Joseph's. It would not be a question merely of two leaders of religious monks differing as to whether it were religiously more perfect to have or not to have monastic possessions, to persecute heretics or to show mercy. Here there was at stake two different concepts of monasticism and the means best adapted to attain personal perfection.

NIL'S SPIRITUALITY

Nil's spirituality exerted a quiet, subdued influence on his generation and on those of the future by his zeal in copying and spreading throughout Russia corrected versions of the writings of the holy Fathers and the lives of the saints. His loyalty to "holy Writings" and the spirit of the Fathers and Mothers of the desert also provided a stronghold of traditionalism in the Trans-Volga region. In his age, when so many of the hierarchy and the princes were desirous of breaking off from dependency on Constantinople and developing a caesaro-papism that made the majority of the hierarchy sycophants to the Tsars, Nil wrote and taught his disciples a universal spirituality of Christianity that flowed directly from the Gospels and apostolic letters and the lives of the holy Fathers of the Church through the early centuries. Nil favored all apostolic links with the early traditions of the Eastern mystics of the early Church. He was adamant about not losing one iota of the traditional teachings of the holy Fathers and the Councils of the Church. In his personal relationship to the heretics of his time, especially the Judaizers and the Strigol'niki (i.e., "Barbers"), he sought to avoid them as much as possible since arguing with them would destroy the environment for proper contemplative prayer. But when one is forced to choose between truth and heresy, Nil exhorts heroism even to martyrdom in defense of truth.

BIOGRAPHY OF NIL

Of all the saints venerated even today in the Russian Orthodox calendar, less is known of the details of St. Nil Sorsky's life than of any other leading saint in Russian history. This no doubt is the result of what legend has told us, namely, that there were lives of St. Nil written up until 1538 when the chronicle reports a conflagration by the "Kazan people," meaning here the Golden Horde.[4] But it is also possible that with the historical developments of the followers of Joseph of Volokolamsk and his type of monasticism victorious under Metropolitan Daniel with the condemnation of the Trans-Volga hermits, followers of Nil, many of the lives of Nil were put to the flames by those who opposed him and his disciples.[5]

But it is certain that we have information leading us to the exact date of his death, May 7, 1508. The only certain details of his life are given in a manuscript of the seventeenth century:

This saintly Father, our Nil, whose parents, who they were, or in what city he was born or in what year he left the world [to be tonsured], we do not know for sure. But we have received something about this from hearsay, that he was born and educated in the Tsar's city of Moscow and there also studied; he received the monk's habit in the Lavra of Kirillo-Belozersky and from there travelled to Constantinople, then to Mount Athos. He then returned to Russia and came under divine guidance to the Sorsky hermitage. And living here some time, pleasing the Lord God with fasting and prayers and struggling against all evils, this holy starets [elder or spiritual guide], the blessed Father, our Nil, fell into eternal sleep in the Lord in the year 7017 [1508], May the 7th. And from here with the good pleasure of God and the prayers of St. Nil, in this hermitage of Sorsky there grew up the skete monastery according to the *Ustav* [*Rule*] and tradition of the holy ancient Fathers.[6]

From a letter written shortly after the death of Nil we learn that his family name was Maikov.[7] It is safe to presume that Nil came from an upper class of educated Russians from his broad travels and his knowledge of Greek and possibly other languages, shown in his writings.

At an early age, he entered the rather strict coenobitic monastery of Kirillo-Belozersky, founded by St. Kirill (†1427).[8] This monastery had two deeply spiritual abbots who no doubt saw the intellectual ability in the young novice and his ardent desire to follow the ancient Fathers of the desert and encouraged him in the reading of what Nil would refer to constantly in his writings as the "holy Writings." This monastery was very rich in the number of manuscripts it possessed.[9]

One of these abbots, Paisy Jaroslavov, full of the Athos ideal, must have guided Nil in his reading of the holy Fathers, especially Nil of Sinai, Symeon the New Theologian, John Climacus, and Gregory of Sinai, who favored the hesychastic view that monks are to strive for continual prayer.[10] To do so they must not be distracted by things of this world, not even to be engaged in agriculture, but they were to occupy themselves with "mental activity" in their cells.

We do not know the time Nil departed for Constantinople and how long he lived on Mt. Athos and possibly also in Palestine. He arrived at Mt. Athos at a time when the hesychastic tradition of asceticism and contemplation, centered around the Jesus Prayer, had reached its highest degree of perfection. He must have been fluent in reading and speaking Greek and thus the riches of the libraries of Mt. Athos and Constantinople furnished him with sources from which he could build a spiritual life in perfect harmony with the highest ideals in Christian Oriental spirituality.

His was evidently more than a mere reading; it must have engaged his whole being, giving him a deep experience of integrated theory and practice that would be seen so clearly in his writings. As a result of "living" rather than merely "studying" the holy Fathers, "he was not chained to their compositions in any exterior manner of repetition, but he freely used them to express his personal thought, but now he thought in a patristic manner and expressed himself in their language."[11]

He returned to his monastery of Kirillo-Belozersky after having spent quite some time in the East.[12] But he found many changes had taken place, not only within himself but also in the general spiritual tenor of the entire monastery. In a letter Nil explains the motives for his leaving the monastery to move to the banks of the stagnant Sora River to establish his hermitage and attract a small number of zealous disciples.[13]

THE SKETE MONASTERY

Nil founded a small community of monks who lived the pure skete rule of life he had lived on Mt. Athos.[14] The skete consisted of a group of cells or huts in which the monks lived. The cells were scattered about a centrally located community church to which the monks came for common liturgical services. The monks lived in groups of two or three, often an older monk and a younger, that is, a starets (elder) with one or two disciples. From the common "cloister" they received food for a week and on Saturday or the vigil of feasts they would come together for services in the church. Each monk lived in a certain sense according to his own needs. He cared for himself, providing his own food and clothing. He set his own daily order and prayer time as he wished.[15]

The order of the skete for Nil and his disciples centered

around continual prayer and the study of the holy Writings. We know that Nil and his monks took up the art of copying manuscripts and also of correcting the glaring errors that existed in many of the manuscripts of an ascetical nature, especially in the lives of the saints. There was no leaving the skete and no preoccupation with the world. A monk's charity toward other human beings was to be shown by his prayers for them and his freely giving of spiritual advice when asked.

NIL'S WRITINGS

In such maximum solitude and intimate communion with his brethren, Nil created his two chief works, his *Tradition* (or in Slavonic, *Predanie*) and his *Ustav* (*Rule*), plus several letters that we have intact today.[16] This book contains a translation of the *Tradition*, the *Rule*, and the letters that we are certain Nil wrote.

The *Predanie* of Nil is his earliest attempt to give his disciples a written but very simplified rule of skete monasticism. Nil's *Tradition* or *Predanie* numbers only nine pages in the critical edition.[17] It was written very early in the life of the skete at the shore of the Sora River. It gives concrete rules and norms of practical conduct for his disciples of the Sorsky skete hermitage. Nil touches briefly on the necessity of following the evangelical tradition as handed down by the holy Fathers; on the need for physical work; on absolute poverty, personal and communal; on obedience to the superior, who should be considered as a brother among other brothers; on rules for eating and drinking; and finally on rules of cloister.

The Rule (Ustav)

One would immediately know by reading a few pages of Nil's main work (numbering eighty pages in the critical edition)[18] that it is not a true rule, such as that of St. Benedict. It really is an extended ascetical treatise on what Nil calls "mental activity," or what we would call today perpetual or continuous prayer. One has the impression of a work tremendously compact, with not a superfluous citation. Only after several readings does the unity of the whole composition appear. By glancing at the chapter headings of this work, we are given a summary not only of Nil's basic teaching in all his written works, including his letters, but also of the key ideas that guided his own drive toward perfection.

INTRODUCTION: From the Writings of the Holy Fathers on Mental Activity

CHAPTERS:

1. Of the various interior (mental) battles waged against us, of the victory and defeat and how one must diligently struggle against the passions.

2. Of our struggle against these mental temptations and how they are to be conquered by the thought of God, through guarding of the heart, that is to say, through prayer and interior tranquillity and how to perform these. Also on spiritual gifts.

3. How and by what means we are to be strengthened in repelling the attacks of mental temptations.

4. On the observation of the common rule in our monastery.

5. On the different ways we must fight and conquer the eight principal temptations of the flesh and others.

6. On all evil temptations in general.

7. On the remembrance of death and the last judgment, how to learn to keep these thoughts ever in our hearts.

8. On tears and how one should act who desires to obtain these.

9. On maintaining the spirit of tears.

10. On renunciation and true freedom from all cares, which consists in dying to all things.

11. On the need to do all these things at their proper time and with becoming moderation and on prayer for these and other needs.

Nil's Letters

There are ten letters attributed to Nil and found in at least one or more manuscripts bearing his name. However, I agree with M. S. Borovkova-Maikova, who clearly proves that only the first four are originals of Nil's own composition. Letters 5 through 10 are merely attributed to Nil's authorship or they are possibly works Nil himself had translated into Slavonic from the original Greek that he may have sent to a disciple living outside his skete monastery. The authentic letters of Nil show us his warmth and love for other human beings, flowing from the affectionate nature of this monk who had left the world in order to love God more and found true charity toward his fellow human beings in his supernatural quest for God alone.

Manuscripts Used for Translation

The *Tradition* and the *Rule* of Nil are sufficiently the same in all the manuscripts that we can be assured of a uniform textual tradition. A scholarly treatment of the 100 manuscripts found in fifteen libraries in Moscow and St. Petersburg was done by M. S. Borovkova-Maikova. She has brought together the most definitive critical text of the two main works of Nil in her critical edition. It is this work, made up of eighty large folios, published in St. Petersburg in 1912, that I have used for my translation of these two works.[19] (PDP) In 1969 I had received a postdoctoral research grant as an exchange professor that allowed me to work in the Lenin Library in Moscow and the Schedrin-Saltykov Library of St. Petersburg (International Research Exchange Board [IREX]). Here I was able to consult the original manuscripts of Nil's writings and other valuable sources not easily available in America. It was principally in Moscow's Lenin Library that I was able to translate the letters of Nil, mainly using the best manuscript available (Troick. Ms. no. 188). Thus all citations of the *Predanie* and *Ustav* of Nil are from M. S. Borovkova-Maikova's critical edition (St. Petersburg, 1912). My translation of Nil's *Last Testament* is also from this edition. My translations of the letters will give the manuscripts used in the endnotes.

THE SPIRITUALITY OF ST. NIL

We must keep in mind the reading audience Nil intended when he composed his two main works and his letters. He was always humbly seeking to share his own wealth of travel, study, and experience of the monastic ideal as he saw it and lived it in the skete form of monasticism. The aim of all the ascetical teachings and practices he gives to his disciples is always union with the indwelling Trinity in this life, as far as grace and the individual's cooperation would allow, and life eternal hereafter. This present life has relevance only in relation to the future, eternal life. It is always a returning to God, who already abides habitually through grace within the baptized Christian.

The goal of all human beings is essentially the same. Individuals, especially monks who have given up all to enter seriously the pursuit of this aim of union with the triune life, have need to use the same means that all holy persons have ever used to attain salvation. For Nil and his monks the first step in the long process of returning to God is to cut oneself off from all extrinsic attachments and then to tie the self to God in one's heart. Such attachment to God demands complete detachment from the world. Nil sums up the goal of monastic life: "Full activity in our chosen way of life should consist in this, that always and in every detail, in every undertaking, in soul and body, word and deed and thought, as far as there is in us the strength, to remain in the work of God, with God, and in God."[20]

Holy Writings, Guide to Perfection

Once a monk divests himself of attachments from the world and its cares, the monk seeks to love God with his whole heart by striving always to do his divine will. This is to be discerned through the traditions given by God's revelation in the teachings of Jesus Christ as found in the Old and New Testaments and in the commentaries and lives of the holy Fathers. "We have but one teacher, our Lord Jesus Christ, who gave us the Holy Scriptures and sent his holy Apostles and venerable Fathers to teach the way of salvation to the human race."[21]

This is the pivotal point of Nil's spirituality: To know the way of perfection leading to God, the Christian must study the holy Writings. He saw this clearly as God speaking in his revelation in Holy Scripture and the holy Fathers interpreting the word of God for us. Not only does one find in these holy Writings the doctrine necessary to be saved, but in all practical difficulties of daily life, one can find the reassurance of what he should do to please God. One is not to search in other sources, for the holy Writings given by God for our salvation are sufficient. The basis for considering the Writings of the holy Fathers as inspired is the sanctity of such early Fathers and Mothers.[22] A monk becomes spiritual by being in living contact with the saints in whom the fullness of the Holy Spirit resides. This contact comes about through their writings or through following a spiritual elder (starets) who is grounded in the holy Writings and lives by their spirit.

Self-Study and Development of the Uniqueness of the Person

One of the features of Nil's spirituality that made him stand out beyond contemporary teachers of the spiritual life, such as Joseph Volokolamsk, is his stress on the principle of self-development. The individual personality of each monk contained the secret of a loving service to God and no mechanical, external obedience alone could ever "extort" this loving submission to God's will. It was the intellect and will developed properly according to God's plan of salvation in the holy Writings that alone could ensure a conscious, active, loving service. The monk had to live evermore conscious of his inner beauty as uniquely loved by the Triune God in and through Jesus Christ and the Holy Spirit. Experiential knowledge of the heart alone could bring about a continual conversion of the individual person in the freedom of surrendering oneself in loving service to God.

The external side of monastic life was reduced to a minimum and the personhood of the monk as the living element became the chief occupation. The externals of the skete life would have meaning only as an expression of the means most suitable to aid the monk's interior life. Perfection for Nil could never consist in mere routine performance of external practices. The monk had to have a conscious understanding of the goal of perfection and the means most suitable to attain it, along with a willing determination to arrive at that end. Therefore, the individual monk had to understand and be convinced of the instructions given him. Then, by force of conviction, he had to put them into practice in his life. So with Nil, as with the ancient Fathers, no step of perfection was reached unless the monk had grasped for himself with his intellect the importance of a given teaching and then with his will moved his whole being to attain the proposed goal by choosing the best means.

Choice of a Spiritual Guide

The second step in the liberation of the true personhood of the monk in the image and likeness of Jesus Christ comes in the important step of choosing his spiritual guide or starets. The elder's oral instructions and example of life will interpret for the younger monk the holy Writings as the voice of God. This choice is most important and a matter of much prayer and discernment to find the suitable man of God as his guide. When no guide can be found, Nil has the monk turn to the Writings and listen to the Lord himself speaking.[23] Nil is handing the monk the words of Christ in Scripture, the writings of the Apostles, the commentaries of the Fathers on these, the writings and the lives of the holy Fathers, and telling him to make these the object of intense study. We can see the high esteem Nil has for a saintly, holy, and intelligent elder to aid the monk in understanding the teachings found in the holy Writings.

The Internal Battle

The spiritual life is conceived by Nil according to the unanimous teaching of all the holy Fathers as a continued internal battle against the evil spirits or forces within the consciousness and the unconscious of the individual. This is not merely a negative process of cutting out the evil presented by the devils to the mind, but also a positive one of encouraging the virtues in imitation of Christ that are supposed to be developed in the battle. In fighting against all the passions, one acquires all the virtues at one time.[24] This is a call to practice what the Greek Fathers called *nepsis*, which means to be inwardly attentive and not carried away as in a spiritual intoxication to the false values of the "world." The first step is to return to God by leaving all worldly attachments and retiring into solitude. Nil writes: "It is characteristic of the strong to draw the sword, the Word of God (Eph 6:14), and struggle in solitude against the demons."[25]

The Psychology of Thoughts

Nil depends on the writings of St. John Climacus in presenting the psychological steps of the development in the mind of an individual thought. These five steps are (1) the presentation or the arising in the mind of a representation, a subject, an image; (2) the coupling or conversation or dialogue with the image; (3) consent given to the thought; (4) slavery to it; and (5) last, passion.[26] On the basis of these steps Nil develops from the holy Writings an analysis of the eight sources of passions. Passions here are not meant as in the usual understanding of the strong emotions called in psychology the irascible and the concupiscible passions. These are rather the principal vices of the soul of which all other temptations are the offspring, that is, gluttony, fornication, covetousness, anger, sadness, acedia, vainglory, and pride.[27]

One's spiritual battle, with much sweat and labor, must consist in the control of the heart, purifying it of every element that might be used by the devil to turn it away from the continual remembrance of God. The end of the interior combat against these passionate thoughts is to expel or at least to weaken them. Only when the heart is freed from these thoughts, when it is "purified," can it begin its ascent to God, to union with him, the end of all spiritual strivings.

NIL'S HESYCHASM

Nil's major contribution to Eastern Christian spirituality lies in the synthesis of the hesychasm of the early Fathers and Mothers of the desert he made in his own personal life and bequeathed to succeeding generations of Russian and neighboring Slavic Christians. This he accomplished through his writings and letters and through the work of his disciples, who continued his form of "heart" spirituality.

The spirituality that Nil learned during his stay on Mt. Athos and brought back to the Russia of his day can best be characterized by the term *hesychasm*.[28] The word comes from the Greek *hesychia*, which means tranquility, peace, calm, or integration of one's true personhood in the heart through contemplative union with Jesus Christ. Hesychasm as a spirituality is a Christian form of living the spiritual life that had its roots in the first hermits who fled into the barren deserts of Egypt and Syria during the fourth century. One author defines hesychasm as a spiritual system of essentially contemplative orientation that finds the perfection of the human person in union with God through continuous prayer.[29] It is far from being a monolithic spirituality, one founded on static elements that have been passed from generation to generation, without any change or addition. However it is defined, hesychasm must not be limited solely to the mechanical recitation of the Jesus Prayer, along with the techniques of respiration, sitting posture, and fixation on the navel. It began as an entire way of life in Christ designed for totally committed Christians striving in the physical deserts to be completely focused in loving surrender on the indwelling Trinity. From such a desert spirituality, hesychasm evolved as it received various influences from spiritual writers representing the Antiochene and Alexandrian schools of thought.

There were historically three schools of writers that brought unique emphasis to hesychasm. The Sinaite school, represented chiefly by Nilus of Sinai, John Climacus, Hesychius of Sinai, and Philotheus, emphasized the solitary life, the guarding of the heart, and mental prayer. They also brought into their writings the "heart" emphasis and the feeling of grace from the writings of Pseudo-Macarius of fourth-century Mesopotamia. The second school of hesychasm is found in the eleventh century in Symeon the New Theologian. The third was centered on Mt. Athos in the fourteenth century, mainly through the efforts of Gregory of Sinai, who started a renaissance of hesychasm with particular emphasis on the Jesus Prayer. When Nil came to Mt. Athos in the fifteenth century, he had free access to a multitude of rich writings on hesychastic spirituality. He was able to read during the years of his stay on Mt. Athos the writings of the hesychastic Fathers in the original Greek or in Slavonic translations made from the Greek writers. Thus he knew the constant teachings of the hesychastic Fathers and all aspects of their spirituality.

Let us sketch these essentials that Nil brought back with him to his native Rus'land.

1. Purity of Heart and Inner Attention

For Nil, the ultimate end of ascetical and mystical endeavor was the union of the individual person with the indwelling Trinity. The means Nil considered absolutely necessary to this end, this intimate union with God through grace and prayer, are the ascetical elements he outlines, both in his two formal treatises and in his letters. Thus we find in his writings, as translated in this volume, continued stress on the traditional themes of the early hesychastic Fathers of the Christian East, such as solitude, silence, control of thoughts, and reaching inner integration on body, soul, and spirit levels. This is known as *hesychia* or tranquility, sobriety, and inner attention (*nepsis* in Greek), achieved especially through the observance of Christ's commandments.

Nil summarizes what he means by solitude in terms of his monks' living strictly the skete type of monasticism: "Isaac gives the following instruction to those desirous to observe true silence and to purify their minds through prayer: 'Retire from the sight of the world and cut off conversations; do not let friends enter your cell, even under the pretext of good intentions, unless they have the same spirit and intention as yourself and are likewise advanced in mystical prayer. Fear mixing with others; against this we can warn from experience. For after we have emerged from intimate conversations, even when they have seemed to be good, our souls are troubled against our will, and these disturbances continue with us for a long time.'"[30]

2. Flight from the World into the Desert

This expression, "flight from the world," Nil uses in the traditional meaning of all the athletes of the desert to refer to the strict living out of the monastic life. In his letter to his disciple, Starets German, Nil recalls his own example of having fled the world and all worldly enticements to devote himself wholly to "living according to the divine writings."[31] Once a monk has separated himself from the world, there must be only one purpose, one dedication: to strive for moral perfection.[32] To Vassian he advises strict withdrawal from talking, hearing, and seeing improper things that could stir up the soul to unrest. "Separate from all who do not live according to the writings of the Fathers."[33]

A monk does not *ipso facto* acquire the necessary purity of heart merely by withdrawing from the world. Strict silence of the heart, exterior and interior, is absolutely necessary. Nil quotes St. Basil on the importance of silence as the beginning of purity of heart: "Strive with active concentration on the task of God alone. St. Basil the Great says that the beginning of purity of heart is silence. And St. John Climacus further defines silence as, first of all, detachment from concern with regard to necessary and unnecessary things; second, as assiduous prayer; and third, as the unremitting action of prayer in the heart."[34]

3. Emptying of Thoughts

Nil, well schooled in the spirituality of the desert Fathers, especially through the writings of Evagrius of the fourth century, insists throughout his writings that to attain contemplative prayer there is need to empty the mind of the multiplicity of thoughts, whether these be good or bad. Nil cites Nilus of Sinai and Hesychius of Jerusalem for his basic teaching on the need to come to "still-pointedness" or "thoughtlessness" in order to be totally focused on God. "Especially should he (the monk) strive to render his mind deaf and dumb in prayer," as Nilus of Sinai says,[35] keeping his heart silent and freed from any thought whatsoever, even should it be a good one, so also says Hesychius of Jerusalem."[36]

Nil exhorts monks who are progressing in contemplative prayer to practice silence, contemplative prayer, and even to avoid the recitation of psalms. Since they are deeply united with the indwelling Trinity, they must guard that the mind not wander away from such union. The emptying of the mind of thoughts is understood only as a result that flows from the degree of detachment from all created beings a monk has in his heart.[37]

Nil summarizes purity of heart as that state of a monk when one possesses nothing, but when, in addition to complete exterior poverty, one has no desire to possess anything.[38]

4. Hesychia

Nil brings nothing new to the traditional hesychastic spirituality that he received from the early Fathers of the desert. He translates the Greek word *hesychia* into Slavonic as *bezmolvie*, which literally means "to be without disturbance, without any agitation."[39] *Hesychia* is more than any mere exterior calm. It indicates an interior state of the soul arrived at through ascetical practices, especially of solitude, silence, and the emptying of the mind and heart not only from all thoughts capable of disturbing the soul during incessant prayer or contemplation, but also from all desires for everyone and everything other than God himself. This is the necessary condition for praying always and for infused union with the indwelling Trinity. This cannot be attained merely by human efforts alone; it necessitates divine assistance along with the monk's inner vigilance and continued ascetical efforts to remain in God's freely given union with the individual monk. It has been well put by Irénée Hausherr: "Hesychasm exists only for prayer and through prayer."[40]

Nil defines the gift of *hesychia* thus: "The fathers call this condition prayer because this gift has its beginnings in prayer and is bestowed on the holy ones during prayer, but no man really knows how to define this phenomenon. When the soul undergoes such spiritual activity and subjects itself completely to God and through direct union nears the Divinity and is enlightened in its movements by an interior light from above and the mind experiences a feeling of future happiness, then it forgets itself, its temporal existence on this earth, and loses any attraction for the things of this earth; There is enkindled in it an ineffable joy, an indescribable sweetness warms the heart, the whole body feels its repercussions and man forgets not only his plaguing passions, but also even life itself and thinks that the Kingdom of Heaven consists of nothing other than this blissful condition."[41]

5. Vigilance and Obeying the Commandments

St. Peter lays the foundational teaching for all the hesychastic teachings and therefore for Nil when he emphasizes the necessity of vigilance. "Be calm but vigilant, because your enemy the devil is prowling round like a roaring lion, looking for someone to eat" (1 Pt 5:8). The patristic teaching on vigilance, which they called by the Greek word *nepsis*, is better described than defined.[42] Throughout his *Ustav* and his other writings, Nil uses over and over two phrases: "mental activity," or similar terms, and the general phrase, "keeping the commandments of God." He quotes Hesychius of Jerusalem in his use of *nepsis* in the most general sense as external and internal vigilance and sobriety. It is synonymous with Evagrius's use of the term *praxis*, which is defined thus: "The practice of virtue (*praxis*) is the spiritual method for purifying the passionate part of the soul."[43]

Nil describes the art of *nepsis* or continued vigilance through a variety of terms, such as "mental activity," or "spiritual exercise," or "prayer of the heart or mind," or "the containing of the mind within the heart, free of all imaginings," or "maintaining the mind in silence." But always he means the same thing. This is the life-giving exercise of guarding the mind in the heart so that no thought may catch the heart unguarded and enter to multiply thoughts and take the soul from union with God.

If the virtue of *nepsis* is the door-keeper, then discretion and moderation are the door through which only the God-pleasing thoughts are allowed to pass into the interior. But when he asks: "What is the norm for judging with proper discretion and prudence every thought, word, deed?," Nil insists on uniting our wills with that of God. Our true love as a return for God's perfect love toward us is to be measured by our effective desire to do the will of God by observing all of the commandments. If we truly love God and wish to surrender ourselves totally to him in return of love, then we will wish to do whatever be the manifest will of God. God wishes always that we live in a loving way so as to share in the trinitarian life dwelling within each Christian.

This is the true proof in the Gospels of our love for God: "If a man has any love for me, he will be true to my word; and then he will win my Father's love and we will both come to him and make our continual abode with him; whereas the man who has no love for me, lets my sayings pass him by" (Jn 14:23–24). Some of these divine commands look only to exterior actions, such as corporal works of mercy. Others are more interior, spiritual. These are more comprehensive, containing in themselves many exterior commands of God. Thus the fulfillment of the interior commands of God ensures the fulfillment also of all the exterior ones. Christ came to give us a new decalogue, the eight Beatitudes, which are the commands of God for all Christians. They center around two interior spiritual commands: to be pure of heart and to be humble of heart.

All virtues are contained in these two, which further narrow down to one all-embracing command: "Love God with your whole soul, your whole heart, and all your strength."[44]

6. Penthos

Nil reflects the universal teaching of the early Fathers of the desert in his teaching on the necessity of a monk's developing the gift of *penthos* or a state of constant compunction or sorrow for past sins. *Penthos* includes a fear of one's inability to save oneself without God's continued mercy that comes to the Christian in humble inner attentiveness and weeping for the continued mercy of God through Jesus Christ.[45] Nil also insists, along with the early Fathers of the desert, on the necessity to meditate on the last things, especially one's own death. We must continually pray for the gift of tears.

Remembering constantly one's death and the Last Judgment does not create a moroseness in the heart of the monk, but rather sets one free to rejoice in the strength of God to do what is impossible for the individual person. Nil sees that the gift of God is always a supernatural and gratuitous one. He writes: "Continue to meditate in this foresaid manner and if God should give us the grace of tears, we must not restrain ourselves, but weep as much as possible, according to our strength and power."[46] The reason why the early Fathers and Nil are in accord on the necessity to weep and to implore God for this gift of tears is found in the effects of tears. "Such tears should be preserved . . . because they have great power and action in destroying and uprooting sins and passions."[47]

7. The Jesus Prayer

Nil explicitly uses the Jesus Prayer as a means to fight temptation. "Our struggle is against these temptations of the mind which are to be vanquished through the remembrance of the thought of God and through the guarding of the heart, that is to say, through prayer and interior silence."[48] The Jesus Prayer as given by Nil consists of the following formulae: "Lord Jesus Christ, Son of God, have mercy on me," or for variation's sake: "Lord Jesus Christ, have mercy on me," or: "Son of God, have mercy on me," or: "Lord Jesus Christ, have mercy on me, a sinner."[49]

It is to be noted with what prudence and reserve, yet with no less fervor and enthusiasm, Nil presents his teaching on this traditional, hesychastic form of incessant prayer. He presents a balanced picture of the Jesus Prayer, especially when he describes the place, time, posture, and manner of reciting it. "Recite the prayer as is most convenient, standing or sitting or reclining, but striving to enclose the mind in the heart. To achieve this, moderate your breathing so as to breathe as seldom as possible, as Symeon the New Theologian teaches."[50] Nil uses this ancient prayer as the best means to combat thoughts, but he also teaches the use of it as the best preparation for what we could call the gift of "infused contemplation," or incessant prayer.

8. Mystical Prayer

Unlike Symeon the New Theologian, Nil never speaks of his own mystical gifts of prayer. He basically is content to teach the higher levels of union with Jesus Christ and the indwelling Trinity through citations of the writings of Isaac the Syrian, Symeon the New Theologian, and Gregory of Sinai. His intention in teaching, especially in his *Ustav*, is not to give his own ideas and personal experiences, but to give the inspired Fathers' teaching on "mental activity."[51]

Nil uses the writings of Isaac the Syrian to describe contemplation, no longer as prayer but as a habitual state beyond any description in human words. He seeks to describe this state thus: "When men experience such ineffable joy, this state suddenly cuts off all vocal prayer from the mouth; the tongue, the heart, the guardian of all thoughts, and the mind, the feeder of feelings, are all silenced, along with the different thoughts that normally soar about like fast-flying birds; now the thought does not govern the prayer, but it itself is directed by another power; it is held in secret captivity and finds itself in confusion, for it dwells on things ineffable and does not know where it is."[52]

To describe what the monk in such mystical prayer experiences during rapturous union with the indwelling Trinity, Nil relies heavily on St. Symeon the New Theologian, the master of mystical description.[53] Nil prudently exhorts the monk who has not received such mystical gifts of prayer not to become discouraged at hearing of the sublime experiences of such mystics as Isaac and Symeon the New Theologian. The monk should always cooperate with grace by offering God a docile will and guarding the heart with continued *praxis*.

Writers Used By Nil

Nil approaches the Fathers much differently from other early Russian spiritual writers, such as his contemporary Joseph Voloko-lamsk. Nil is not concerned with finding in the Fathers an authority to substantiate his own teaching, but he quotes them principally as a disciple quotes a master. He tells his reader over and over that what he writes is not his own, but that it is doctrine taught and lived by the Fathers. His purpose is not to give new, original ideas of his own, but to be faithful to the teachings of the Fathers, for their writings are "the waters of life" that will quench human concupiscences and guide men to the truth.[54]

Among the Fathers serving as a source of Nil's spirituality one can distinguish two categories. First are the Fathers Nil quotes often and to whom he is evidently more inclined in regard to their general lines of spirituality. These include St. John Climacus, Isaac the Syrian, Gregory of Sinai, and Symeon the New Theologian. Second are Fathers who are quoted a few times directly or cited only implicitly, but whose ideas influenced Nil's thought.

Taking his two main literary works, we can readily see which Fathers were for Nil his favorite sources of spirituality. He quotes thirty-one patristic writers, but the names frequently repeated are few. The numbers in parentheses indicate how many times Nil quotes a given writer in his two works: Climacus (35); Isaac the

Syrian (33); Gregory of Sinai (27); Symeon the New Theologian (18); Basil the Great (10); Barsanuphius (8); Nil of Sinai (6); Philotheus of Sinai (5); John Chrysostom (4); Ephrem the Syrian (4); Hesychius of Sinai (4); Peter Damascene (3); Maximus Confessor (3); Dorotheus (2); Arsenius (2); Nicetas Stethatos (2); Macarius (2); Anthony (2); Daniel the Hermit (2); Gregory the Great, Pope of Rome (2); John Damascene (2); Pachomius (1); Agathon (1); Symeon the Studite (1); Mark the Hermit (1); Diadochus (1); Theodore the Studite (1); Gregory Nazianzen (1); Andrew of Crete (1); Germanus, Patriarch of Constantinople (1); Eugenia Martyr (1).[55]

Nil's Independence in Using the Holy Writings

Although the Fathers are directly or indirectly quoted in Nil's *Predanie* and *Ustav* in various places, we can say that his ideas are all patristic, for that is his very purpose. But even in these two works Nil manifests a great deal of independence and originality. There is little doubt that Nil was a strong-willed personality, revealed especially in his letters. This trait, added to his intellectual acumen and practical knowledge of the Fathers' writings, makes his single purpose in writing stand out clearly before the reader. All other considerations are accidental and subordinated to the final end he has in mind.

His purpose in the *Ustav* is to present the doctrine of the Fathers on the mental battle, on the means necessary to conquer the devil in the individual's heart through constant mental (interior) prayer, and on living in the permanent presence of God, totally supple to his holy will. With this purpose in mind, Nil marshals his patristic texts in admirable unity and singleness of scope. Thus the *Ustav* appears to be a carefully laid out mosaic, producing a composite picture of great unity and consistent teaching.

Nil shows his individuality in his interpretation of the spiritual life and the rule of asceticism through his stress of the "battle" motif. He never cites the Fathers except insofar as they are witnesses to some phase of this master idea.

Nil also shows independence from his sources, especially from his favorite authors (Climacus, Cassian, and Nil Sinaite), in his avoidance of any legendary elements. He offers us practically no examples of the things that these Fathers so abounded in—no metaphors, aphorisms, and rhetorical figures of speech. He uses their psychological interpretation of temptations and the eight passions, but only as a practical means to an integrated battle against any obstacle to union with the divine will. One has the impression that not one quotation from the Fathers is superfluous. Thus we see that Nil has thought out his plan for a very long time and has become thoroughly convinced of the necessity of his theme. No one could ever accuse him of being a mere compiler of patristic sayings. His ordering of these sayings is too original and too independent. The end result is a new creation, and for Russian spirituality, a work of great value.

Appraisal of Nil as Hesychast

Nil is the first important hesychast writer in Russia. Earlier Russian authors, like Dositheus the Archimandrite of Kiev and Athanasius Rusin, knew the hesychast asceticism and the Jesus Prayer from their stay on Mt. Athos, yet as A. S. Orlov affirms: "It is well known that Nil observes more faithfully in his *Ustav* the testimonies of the Byzantine hesychasts, even in the details of expressions."[56] Nil works into a synthetic treatise of great balance that which would otherwise have remained scattered throughout various *florilegia* or collections of patristic sayings. In this manner he not only bequeaths to Russian spirituality and monasticism a solid asceticism, but he blends the two leading lines of spirituality that in his times had influenced the whole Byzantine world—the spirituality of Evagrius along with that of Macarius, Diadochus, and Symeon the New Theologian.

Evagrius with his faithful followers, Isaac the Syrian and John Climacus, stressed pure intellectual contemplation. The whole of asceticism was aimed at delivering the monk from the passions to arrive at the *apatheia*,[57] where the soul would be able to return to the

31

"primitive state" of Adam before the fall and find and contemplate God, purely, without any images, without any thought. The line of Pseudo-Macarius and his followers kept the strict asceticism of Evagrius with its stress on solitude and silence, and the emptying of the mind of all thoughts, striving for *hesychia*, but they also added the heartfelt element.[58] The heart became the place where the mind contemplated God. To the external ascesis was added the interior one of "weeping" at the thought of death and the Last Judgment, and of remaining in this interior spirit of compunction or *penthos* as a means of purifying the heart from the influences of the passions. When the mind descends into the interior regions of the heart, the fruition of this ascesis, or *praxis* as Evagrius calls it, is had in the continual contemplation of God within the heart. This is achieved by the use of the Jesus Prayer both as a means to grow in purity of heart and as a preparation for purer contemplation. It is this combination of spiritual traditions that Nil made available to Russia and the Slavic world.

Influence of Nil

Every culture and every nation undergoes at certain times radical changes. History shows that Providence provides leaders that appear on the scene to effect such great changes that impact a nation for all of its future. Nil Sorsky and Joseph Volokolamsk were two such spiritual leaders who appeared on the religious stage in a drama that played itself out in the latter part of the fifteenth and the beginning of the sixteenth centuries in Russia.[59] Unfortunately, Russian historians have often tended to present the complexities of this turbulent time in Russia's early religious history in simplistic, oppositional categories. Nil is usually presented as the leader of a type of skete monasticism that emphasized only the contemplative life, interior freedom, inner conscious convictions in a Spirit-filled intellectualism, mercy shown toward heretics, and evangelical poverty with social protest against the contemporary abuses of rich monastic possessions. Joseph is presented in opposite terms as a monk greatly involved in various social apostolates, stressing external obedience to the letter of the law with sycophantic obedience to the Tsar, favoring the death penalty for all heretics and the absolute need of monastic holdings to carry on the religious vocation.[60] This is far too simple a picture.

I have pointed out that Nil's main desire was to live the hidden skete type of monastic life in union with his small band of disciples.[61] Therefore, we do not find a claim in history books that he had a great influence on the religious or political levels of Russian life at that time. We do find in such books Gennadius, archbishop of Novgorod, who was involved in eradicating the heresy of the Judaizers of northern Russia, imploring Joasaf, archbishop of Rostov, in whose diocese Nil and his mentor at the Kirillo Monastery lived, to come and help him deal with this problem. "Write to me if it is possible for Paisy and Nil to come to me and to discourse with me about the heretics [i.e., the Judaizers]."[62] Nil also made a vehement protest in the Moscow Synod of 1503 against the monasteries's holding huge properties through currying the favor of the Tsar and the wealthy boyars and princes. He felt such monasteries sold out their evangelical following of true poverty as befits authentic monks. "And when there was held the council about widowed priests and deacons, the Starets Nil got up and said that monasteries should not have villages, but monks should live in solitude and be fed by the fruit of their own hands. And with him were all the hermits of the Belozersky region."[63] So Nil, although he desired a life of hidden prayer, was not afraid to take a public stand on issues that involved the purity of the faith and of the monastic life.

INFLUENCE ON HIS DISCIPLES

Nil retired to his monastery after the Moscow Synod and five years later he died. But his intervention had repercussions for centuries as his disciples continued to fight the worldliness and rich possessions of the monasteries under the influence and teaching of Joseph Volokolamsk. This later group, especially under Metropolitan Daniel, eventually burned most of the hermitages of the Transvolgian hermits and most of the writings of Nil's disciples.[64]

Some of Nil's disciples, such as Prince Vassian Patrikeev, Maxim the Greek, Kassian, Artemy, Paul Obnora, Prince Andrei Zaozersky, Dimitry Prilucky, Dionisy Glushicky, Gregory Pelsemsky, and many others, by their writings and example, carried on the teachings of Nil. The chief disciple of Nil's school of thought, who engaged directly in this struggle with Joseph and his followers, was Prince Vassian Patrikeev, who was forced to take the tonsure by order of the Tsar Ivan III, after having been implicated in a political scandal.[65] From his polemic writings against Joseph, we can see the impact of Nil's influence upon Vassian. In pleading for mercy in governmental and ecclesiastical dealings with heretics, Vassian used Nil's emphasis on the infinite mercy of God. He insisted that the mercy of God posits the universal will of God to save all sinners by bringing them to repentance.[66] There is no sin that cannot be pardoned if the sinner repents, but, he argues, "those who put the heretics to death without a chance to repent, make of them martyrs."

I have detailed in another work[67] other disciples who were inspired by the writings of Nil on the skete form of monasticism. As representative of another disciple typical of those who faithfully lived their monastic lives according to Nil's principles, we find the outstanding disciple Artemy. In his writings he clearly presents Nil's strict views on monastic asceticism, stressing Nil's totality and dedication to the contemplative life with absolute detachment from the world.

Nil was not developing a new brand of Christian monastic spirituality that could not have been found in early Russia before his time. But his importance, as seen in his writings and in those of his followers, is that he formulated in an organized manner that same tradition that his beloved hesychastic Fathers of the Sinaite and Mt. Athos tradition had passed on to the early saints of Russian monasticism. Saints Anthony and Theodosius of the Kievan Pechersky Lavra, Abraham of Smolensk, Metropolitan Kiprian, Sergei Radonezh, Paul Obnora, and Kirill Belozersky, along with so many other hidden names had lived this similar hesychastic life, but had lacked the patristic learning to synthesize this tradition in an orderly composition. The many followers of Nil disseminated the key ideas of Nil's hesychastic synthesis, incarnating them in the biographies of saints they wrote. Nil's ideas became the common patrimony of the Russian and other Slavic peoples.

Nil's greatest influence would always come from his two main works, *Predanie* and *Ustav*, which were copied out by hand and passed from monastery to monastery, from house to house. It is estimated that today there are over 150 manuscripts still extant of these two works.

When Joseph's ideal of a symphony between church and state came crashing down under the autocratic secular fist of Peter the Great, there were still monks in Russia and abroad who were influenced by Nil's writings. Nikodim of Mt. Athos in the nineteenth century collected in his *Philokalia* the hesychastic Fathers who formed Nil's spirituality, and Paisy Velitchkovsky of Moldavia translated the *Philokalia* into Slavonic and called it the *Dobrotolubie* (Love of the Good). Nil's writings complemented the selections found in the *Dobrotolubie* so that his name was always revered by the Russian monks in subsequent centuries and even by the simple people, while Joseph Volokolamsk has remained a name in history books relegated to the fifteenth and sixteenth centuries.

Nil Sorsky's influence on Orthodox monasticism is especially evident in Paisy Velitchkovsky. Although circumstances forced him to remain in Moldavia, where he directly launched a revival of Nil's skete form of monasticism, he can be called the father of the modern Russian contemplative tradition. Through his translation of the *Philokalia* from Greek to Slavonic he gave a great impetus to interior prayer and hesychastic spirituality throughout Russia. Paisy wrote an *Ustav* or *Rule* that is made up of eighteen parts, many[68] of which contain texts and ideas quoted from Nil and his sources. M. S. Borovkova-Maikova, whose texts of Nil's writings I have used in these translations, provides a critical comparison of these two *Ustavs* and concludes:

The repetition of ideas and even exact words of Nil, the remembrance of him, all taken together, give us the impression not only of the influence of Nil on his near successors, but also on a man who lived 200 years later and thousands of miles away. Both strove to renovate monasticism. Naturally we do not deny the immediate influence of Athos on Paisy, but we say that the striking resemblance in the two compositions and the close acquaintance through writings of the young man with the Starets Nil and his evident interest in the latter give us the right to think that the influence of Nil was more than that of Athos.[69]

It would be impossible to measure what influence the writings of Nil have on present-day Russian and other Slavic monasteries, so soon after the breakdown of Soviet Russia and the communist rule found in other Slavic countries. One concluding testimony of Nil's continuing influence can be found in the appreciation of the timeliness of Nil's spirituality for Russian and other Slavic émigrés, not only for monks, but also for laypersons. In 1958 the Pochaevsky Press in Montreal, Canada, reprinted the edition of Bishop Justin's life of Nil and a summation of his *Ustav*.[70] In Bishop Vitaly's short preface we can see the ongoing influence of Nil Sorsky and his writings for persons who in our modern world still hunger and thirst to live a life of deeper, contemplative prayer, one that focuses them totally on conscious living for the glory of God:

Instead of understanding the significance of the Gospels and going to him who with a single word healed the possessed boy of Gerasa, there has appeared an innumerable quantity of psychoanalysts, who, by means of very doubtful principles based on the half-atheistic philosopher Freud, attempt to substitute for the Holy Sacrament of Confession. . . . In the following composition of St. Nil Sorsky there is unfolded the simplest teaching of Christ's Church about the development of every kind of sin. By this teaching each person can, with surprising clarity, see how sin, the cause of all unhappiness in general and of all sufferings, of all mental disturbances and abnormalities, is conceived. One can follow the path it takes in the human soul, and, most important of all, each person, in

this unfolding of wisdom, can see his own personal relationship to the truth, to the God-Man who gave us an
eternal example of the only genuine norm.[71]

CONCLUSION

The sad history of Russian spirituality is that in the sixteenth
century a choice was offered between the simple evangelical spirituality of Nil Sorsky and the accommodated Christianity of Joseph
Volokolamsk. The religious leaders and the Tsars chose to follow
the aegis of Joseph, with his emphasis on external ritualism, monastic possessions, and the Church in submission to the Tsar, the
Christian Prince, who not only guided the destinies of All-Russia,
but of the Third Rome. When Tsar Peter the Great forgot his
Christian duties, he found little opposition to his plans for wiping
away the Patriarchate and setting up his own autocratic Synod to
guide the Church as he politically saw fit. When the last Tsar was
removed in the twentieth century by the Communist Revolution,
the Third Rome came tumbling down and the chauvinistic Mes-
sianism of the Slavophiles disappeared amidst the rubble. We may
wonder whether the destiny of Russia and our modern world would
have been different had both of the conflicting spiritualities of the
sixteenth century been allowed equal development, that is, if Nil's
spirituality had been allowed to continue to develop hermitages
faithful to the deeply desert spirituality of the holy Fathers alongside the more social-slanted spirituality of Joseph Volokolamsk.

1. The Tradition (*Predanie*)

This is the tradition of the elder, Nil, hermit, to his disciples and to all who may find it to their liking concerning the skete-type of life as found in the writings of the holy Fathers.

With the help of our Lord God and Savior and his most pure Mother, I have written a composition to benefit my own soul and those of my lords, who are my closest brothers, one in spirit and not to be considered as my disciples.[1] I consider you not as my disciples. For we have only one Teacher, our Lord, Jesus Christ, the Son of God, who has given to us the Sacred Scriptures. He is the one who taught and sent the holy Apostles and venerable Fathers to teach the way of salvation to the human race. These disciples first performed good and then they instructed others. But as for me, I have not accomplished any good toward anyone, but I explain the holy Writings to those who eagerly seek to be saved.

There have been some who came to me that I may instruct them in the Writings and live here my style of life, but I sent them away, for I myself am a sinful and ignorant person with many infirmities of soul and body. Yet those whom I have rejected give me no rest and continually return to harass me. This is a great distress to me. And for this reason I have taught the holy Writings on behalf of the Lord and for the salvation of my brothers and all who wish to learn how to lead a better life by turning away from an evil life. Yet there are those who with carnal wisdom and the examples of the worldly and vain ones try to undermine our life-style as enemies in our midst. These seek to destroy our life that we live according to the holy Writings and the teachings of the Fathers.

We must be grounded in the tenets of our faith. I believe in one God, in the glorious Trinity of the Father and the Son and the Holy Spirit, one in being and undivided. I believe also in the incarnation of the Son of God who is both truly God and truly man. I profess this and all the other creeds of the Orthodox Church and accept and confess with all my soul. Also with great faith and love I profess that my Lady is the holy, most pure Birth-Giver of God and I exalt and glorify her.

And I respect and accept all the saints and I exalt them and unite myself with them by the grace of Christ. I also have recourse with all my soul to the holy, catholic, and apostolic Church. And I accept all its teachings which the Church hands down from the Lord and the holy Apostles and holy Fathers of the ecumenical and local councils and from the other holy Fathers, all of which form the Tradition passed down concerning the Orthodox Faith and the decrees of the church councils.

All these I accept and reverence with great faith and love.

I see clearly that if it is God's will for us to gather together, then it behooves us to live according to the traditions of the saints and fulfill the commands of God and observe the traditions of the holy Fathers and not to excuse ourselves by ignoring the blame of sins by saying that nowadays it is impossible to live according to the Scriptures and follow the Writings of the holy Fathers.

But if we also are weak, still it is proper to follow the example of the ancient and blessed Fathers, even if we are not able to equal their exploits. If anyone does not wish to follow this basic approach, let him cease harassing me, even though I also am a poor sinner. I turn away such persons and have nothing to do with them.

I do not wish to be their master, and still they come and try to force me to lead them. Also for those who live together with us, if they do not care to observe our teaching which I give them from the holy Writings, I do not wish to answer for them, for I am not guilty for their self-will. But for those who really desire to live our style of life freely and without any worldly thinking, I accept such. I teach them the word of God, even though I myself do not always perfectly observe it, and I pray that by the grace of Christ through the prayers of those who have profited by my teaching, I am able to be compared to those described by St. Climacus:[2] "Men sunk in a mud hole can warn passers-by of their imminent danger, and for the sake of those thus saved, may our Lord also deliver the fallen." And again he says: "Do not seek proudly to judge in teaching disciples, especially in the case of those who are lazy." And again he exhorts that "we should fear the sins of the recalcitrant ones." Also St. Maximus teaches in a similar fashion: "There are many who speak much, but produce little."[3]

But no one should be neglectful to observe the word of God, but he should confess his own weakness and not cover up God's truth. In this way we will not be guilty of any crime against the commands and words of God by speaking in this way. For such are the words of the holy Fathers and according to them we, by searching out the holy Writings, pass them on to those who come to us and seek such teachings. We, however, unworthy though we are, do not hide the writings of the blessed Fathers on Sacred Scripture and carefully teach them to those who dwell with us, which always brings a great danger.

Violators of these Traditions

If any one of the brothers should fall away from these traditions out of sloth or carelessness, he should have to confess such violations to the elder and in this way the elder can correct his fault. And this should be done if the violation is committed in his cell or outside of it. It is a great danger to be found outside of the cell and, therefore, a monk must be extremely cautious to observe all the precepts. But there are many who hate to give up their own will instead of doing the will of God, but then they deceitfully seek to justify themselves with lies.

Concerning such persons, St. John Climacus says: "It is better to dismiss those than to allow them to do their own will. For by sending such a person away, you will humble him and show him how to give up doing his own will. But if under the pretense of showing him brotherly love, you are indulgent to him, you will be cursed by him at the hour of his death."

This instruction has been handed down to us from the holy Fathers that we are to earn our daily food and other necessities by proper labors with our hands and our work, as the Lord and his most holy Mother have commanded us to do. St. Paul says that whoever does not work, does not eat.[4]

A Monk's Work

Our style of living and our needs are found legislated for us in such sources. Such work must be done inside the cell. For the holy Writings tell us that monks living in a coenobitic monastery may plow with a pair of oxen in the open fields, yet this is condemned for hermits. If we are unable to supply for our needs from our own work, because of our physical weakness, or for any other valid reason, we may receive a small amount of alms from Christ-loving persons, but only for what is needed, never any excessive amounts.

It is forbidden that by force we receive from the fruit of others' labors, for that would not be in keeping with our goal. For how can we observe the command of the Lord while possessing such goods? "If someone will contest you and take away your coat, give him also your cloak."[5]

We are victims to our passions and very weak, but we must run away from and avoid the desire to possess such earthly things, avoiding such possessions like death-dealing poison.

In the buying of our necessities and in the selling of our artifacts, it befits us not to haggle with a brother to his disadvantage, but rather we should be ready to receive less even than what would be just. So also if we hire laypersons, we should never withhold what is owed them, but give them their just due and with our blessing send them off in peace. It is not proper for us to possess any superfluities. In regard to giving alms to those who beg of us and lending, do not be disturbed, for, as Basil the Great says, this is not demanded of a monk, since he has nothing beyond his own needs and is not obliged to give such alms.[6]

Possessing Nothing and Giving Alms

And if one should say "I have nothing," he is not lying, as St. Barsanuphius the Great says.[7] "For a monk is exempt from giving alms. He can sincerely say: 'We have given up everything to follow you, the Lord.'" St. Isaac writes: "Not to possess anything is higher than giving alms."[8] The alms of a monk are to help a brother by a saving word given in time of need and to offer spiritual discernment, to comfort another in time of sorrow or any other need. But this applies to monks who are able to give such to others.

In regard to novices, as St. Dorotheus says: "Their patience in bearing with trials, insults, and rebukes inflicted upon them by their brothers is a more spiritual alms of a superior order than any mere material alms, just as the soul is superior to the body."[9]

If a stranger should come to us, let us put him at ease as best we can. And when we give bread if he has asked us, give it with your blessing and then let us be permitted to depart.

In Leaving the Hermitage

In regard to our leaving our hermitage, this should not be done simply as a personal indulgence, but rather in accord with our established rules and for a necessary reason. It is not fitting for us to leave our cells without a reason and a blessing, as St. Basil the Great says: "It is up to the superior to assign to a brother his special task. Thus he may order an individual monk to be sent on various assignments as he discerns. The monk who receives such an assigned task should not violate his obedience to God by making the assignment an occasion for laxity, but with the fear of God and with great care, carry it out for his own good and that of others."

All that I have written here I wish to be observed while I am living and also after my death. In our cells it is fitting that the brothers and strangers who visit us should be instructed by those monks of proven virtue and ability to direct souls. They should be skilled in the art of listening and in giving helpful counsel. All these things that I have written are to be carried out as far as they are pleasing to God and helpful to souls. If such are not done, let us do something better that is more pleasing to God and helpful for souls.

ADORNMENTS OF THE CHAPEL

Concerning the adornments of churches, St. John Chrysostom writes: "If anyone should wish to donate sacred utensils or any other adornment for the church, tell him to distribute his money to the poor for no one has ever been judged for not decorating the church."[10] And other saints say the same thing. St. Eugenia the martyr also, when sacred silver vessels were offered to her, said: "It is not fitting for a religious in a monastery to have silver possessions."[11] For this reason it is not fitting that we also should possess gold and silver objects, not even for sacred vessels and other unnecessary adornments except to have only the bare necessities for the church.

Pachomius the Great would not even allow the very structure to be adorned.[12] After he had constructed the church of the Mochos monastery with beautiful brick pillars, he then thought that it was not proper to admire the beauty wrought by human hands and thus be puffed up by the beauty of the building. So he tied ropes around the pillars and ordered the brethren to pull with all their strength in order to make the pillars to lean and destroy their beauty. He said: "This was done so that our mind, so prone to subtle praises, will not be ensnared by the devil through vainglory." So if such a great saint spoke and acted in this way, how much more it is fitting for us, who are so weak and enslaved by our passions, to be protected against such things.

CONCERNING FOOD AND DRINK

What concerns food and drink, let each one accommodate himself to his physical and spiritual strength, always avoiding satiety and gluttony. In regard to intoxication, we ought not to drink any liquid that should induce such a state. Those who are young and healthy ought to discipline their bodies by fasting and going thirsty and by hard work as much as they can. Let the older and infirm be content with doing little.

We must not have in our own possession in our cells any dishes or any objects of great value and beauty. So also the structure of the hermitage and other buildings of the skete monastery should be built of cheap and unadorned materials, as Basil the Great says, namely, that the building materials should be easily found everywhere and purchased at low cost. Women should not be allowed to enter our skete nor should we have any female beasts of burden for work or any other purpose. Also there should not be allowed any beardless youths in our service and we should avoid any beardless and feminine-looking youth.

2. The Monastic Rule (*Ustav*)

Introduction: From the writings of the holy Fathers on "mental activity." In what does its profit consist? How carefully ought we to strive to develop it? Written by the Elder Nil.

Many of the holy Fathers have discoursed on "heart activity" and "guarding of the spirit" and "mental attentiveness," in their various teachings as they received inspiration from God's grace. But they all understood these teachings which they have received from the Lord himself who said: "Out of the heart flow evil thoughts which defile a person." Therefore we are taught to cleanse the inner vessel, and, as he says, we must in spirit and in truth adore God.[1] In this matter the Fathers hand down the statement from the Apostles that, if I pray only with my tongue or lips, but my spirit is not praying, it is my voice praying while my mind is fruitless. But if I pray with my spirit, I also pray with my mind. And this is affirmed by my witness of the Apostle [St. Paul] on "mental prayer," where we read this saying: "I would wish to say with my mind five words rather than a thousand words with my tongue."[2]

St. Agathon says: "Bodily action is like a leaf. Interior action, namely, spiritual striving, is the fruit." Terrible is the indictment in the sayings of the saints in this matter: "Every tree not producing good fruit (which is spiritual attentiveness) shall be cut down and cast into the fire." And again the Fathers teach that if prayers are only on the lips, but the spirit is not involved, it is as though prayer is being offered to the air. God pays attention only to the spirit praying. St. Barsanuphius the Great says: "If interior action does not accompany a person praying with God's help, he labors all in vain in his exterior actions."[3]

St. Isaac also teaches: "Bodily action divorced from the spiritual is similar to sterile loins and dry breasts since God's wisdom cannot approach it."[4] And many other holy Fathers teach the same and are in total agreement on this point. Blessed Philotheus of Sinai[5] speaks of certain monks who, because of their lack of experience, settle for doing good works, but are ignorant of the spiritual combat, the victories and defeats, since they ignore the mind. He counsels us to pray for such monks and to teach them in order that they may protect themselves against evil actions and that they may purify their mind, which is the mirror of the soul.

In former times it was not only the holy Fathers who lived as hermits in the desert in solitude with spiritual discipline who received grace and *apatheia*[6] and purity of soul. This discipline was attained also by those monks dwelling in coenobitic monasteries, but also those monks not removed from the world who dwelt even in cities, as Symeon the New Theologian and his elder [starets], Symeon the Studite[7] who lived in the large Studite monastery in the large and populated city of Constantinople, who shone like stars through their spiritual gifts.

Such also were Nikita Stethatos and many others. The same teaching comes from blessed Gregory of Sinai[8] that not only hermits living in solitude practice attention and hesychasm[9] and mental discipline, but also monks living in coenobitic monasteries. They all can devote themselves to inner attentiveness. And all such holy ones discovered the grace of the Spirit by observing the commandments, first those that govern the emotions, then the spiritual levels. Without such discipline no one will find this amazing and wonderful gift, as the holy Fathers have taught. Blessed Hesychius of Jerusalem[10] says: "Just as it is not possible to preserve this natural life of ours without eating and drinking, so it is impossible to attain any spiritual perfection without guarding the mind, which is called also 'being sober,'[11] even for those who valiantly struggle to avoid sinning seriously out of fear of the pains of hell."

Importance of a Spiritual Guide

Symeon the New Theologian says this great and most beautiful and irridescent work is often imparted to many through instruction. Yet there are some who acquire it directly from God by their ardent faith. In a similar way Gregory of Sinai and other saints concur. They insist that it is not an easy task to find a skilled and trustworthy guide in this wonderful discipline. For, they explain, such a trustworthy instructor must have much personal experience and be grounded in the wisdom of the holy Writings. He must also have acquired the gift of spiritual discernment.

Even in the time of those saints we are told that such a teacher was not easily found. In our present time of such evil all the more diligence must be had in seeking such a guide. But if such a teacher cannot be found, they, the saintly Fathers, order us to study the Sacred Scriptures and hear our Lord himself speaking: "Search the Scriptures and in them you will find eternal life." For St. Paul the Apostle says that all that was written in the Sacred Scriptures was written for our instruction (cf. Rom 15:4). Thus the saints, who underwent great discipline to control their feelings and labored in mental prayer in the vineyard of their own heart and purified their mind of all passions, have discovered the Lord and attained spiritual wisdom. We, too, who are so enflamed by the fires of our passions, are enjoined to draw the living water from the fountain of the Sacred Scriptures, which have the power to extinguish the fires of our passion and instruct us in the understanding of the truth.

For this reason, even though I am a great sinner and not endowed with wisdom, I also assiduously have applied myself to the holy Writings according to the inspired Fathers' teachings. Like a slave I was imprisoned by unbecoming passions, which are the basic roots of evil in all things. Thus it is not because I have overcome the passions in a healthy, benevolent silence, but because of my sickness of the passions that I have collected together a little out of what I found from the holy Writings. Like a dog picking up crumbs that fall from the table, so I have gathered together the words of those blessed Fathers and have written all this to be a reminder to us to imitate them, even if it be only in an insignificant way.

Contents

The contents of these writings deal in general with the following topics: How a monk should properly engage in this "mental" work provided he truly wishes to be saved in these times. How he can and ought to deal with his thoughts and feelings according to the holy Writings and the lives of the holy Fathers.

Table of Contents

I. Of the Various Spiritual Battles Waged Against Us; Our Defeats and Victories and How to Battle Strenuously Against the Flesh.

Discourse One of the Elder, Nil the Hermit, on the Five Steps of a "Thought" Leading to Captivity *or* Passion.

The Fathers speak of a variety of wars in which the mind must engage with accompanying victories and defeats. First, there is the presentation of the thought [*prilog*]; then the dialogue with the suggestion; then the acceptance of it; then the enslavement and lastly the passion.[12]

a. THE SUGGESTION

The *suggestion*, the holy Fathers say (e.g., John Climacus and Philotheus of Sinai and others), is a simple thought or image about some object or happening that we carry in our heart and that appears as a thought in our mind. Gregory of Sinai says that such a thought can arise through the suggestion of the devil, who tempts us to do this or that, as he tempted Christ, our God: "Command these stones to become bread" (Mt 4:3).

Simply stated, this is an ordinary thought that flits through the human mind. And such a thought, the Fathers say, is neither sinful nor praiseworthy nor even instructive in itself. For it is impossible for us to prevent the presence of the enemy's thoughts, as Symeon the New Theologian says: "The devil and his demons, who were driven out of heaven by God because they failed to obey God when they were tempted, find an entrance into a person."

b. DIALOGUING

Dialoguing or entertaining a thought, as the Fathers say, takes place when a thought or phantasm has been suggested by the enemy and the person with passion or no passion freely entertains the thought as he carries on a seeming conversation with the thought. In a word, he plays with the thought in the mind as he reflects upon it. This, the Fathers say, is not always without sin. However, it can become meritorious if it is used as an occasion to please God. If a person does not cut off the initial presentation of the evil thought, but begins to dialogue with it and the enemy entices him to think of it with passion, let him then take care to change it into something good. How we are to accomplish this by changing the thought into a good one, with God's help, we will later explain.

c. CONSENTING TO THE SUGGESTION

Consenting, as the Fathers teach, is when the sensual part of the soul is inclined toward the proposed thought or image—in a word, when a person accepts the thought or image presented by the enemy, and not only entertains it but moves in some way to actuate the proposed thought.

The Fathers say that the guilt in accepting the thought depends on the level of spiritual advancement acquired. If a person has progressed to the degree of accepting God's help to drive away such thoughts, yet becomes lazy and does not take care to drive away evil thoughts, such a one will not be without sin. If, however, one is a beginner and not very strong in the spiritual life to resist such suggested evil, such a person, if he yields a bit to such a thought but yet confesses at once to the Lord and calls on his name, being repentant as he reproaches himself, God will forgive him through his divine mercy on account of his human weakness.

This is the teaching of the Fathers on "entertaining" thoughts. It means that a person unwillingly is defeated while struggling with the thought, yet the center of his soul is firmly fixed, resolved not to sin and not to do any evil act. As Gregory of Sinai says: "It even happens that amidst the passion and in the struggle against the presented thoughts, as St. Isaac says, one willingly accepts the thoughts of the enemy and dialogues with the thoughts and is overcome by them. He then stops resisting the passion and he resolves to commit the sin. Now even if he is prevented from doing the action either because of the circumstances of time or place or for any other reason, his sin is a grievous one and he is subject to join those excommunicated."

d. CAPTIVITY

In regard to *captivity* or *enslavement*, this can be either a necessary and unwilling distraction of the heart or a persistent preoccupation with certain thoughts destructive to our calling. Such a thought can be unavoidable and not willed when the mind is taken captive by a thought or phantasm and led into evil designs against one's will, but with God's help, that person is able to return to himself. But the second type of captivity occurs when we find ourselves buffeted about by waves in a storm. We are carried away from our own good intentions toward evil thoughts and we cannot return to our calm and peaceful disposition. This comes about often by frequent and unprofitable conversations, which are very destructive and take us away from our noble disposition.

The first type of enslavement is judged by whether it occurs in time of prayer or outside of prayer and whether it is occasioned by thoughts of an inferior nature or of an intrinsically evil nature. If the mind becomes enslaved or is taken captive by evil thoughts during prayer, this is a very grievous sin. The mind in time of prayer should be alert and turn away from all kinds of such thoughts. But if such a temptation occurs outside of prayer and while we pursue concerns necessary to our existence, such is not a sinful matter for even the saints themselves performed works essential to their living situation. The Fathers teach that regardless of what be our thoughts, if the mind is turned inwardly in a pious attitude, it is one with God. We must always turn away from all evil thoughts.

e. PASSION

The second type of captivity, as the Fathers truly call it, "passion," is when after a long time a certain thought becomes nested within the soul, and, like a habit, becomes a part of a person's own nature. He has freely allowed it to enter within himself so now he is continually disturbed by carnal thoughts inspired by the enemy. Repeatedly a phantasm is presented to the troubled soul, which is willy-nilly attracted to it more than to all other thoughts.

Now this happens as a result of carelessness when a person carries on a dialogue and willingly consents to surrender to improper thoughts. This sin demands either repentance in proportion to its seriousness or torments in the future life. In a word, we need to repent and pray for deliverance from such passion. For our future torment will be doled out according to our failure to repent and not by the fact that we were tempted. If this were so, then no one could be forgiven unless he would be perfectly without any passions, as Peter Damascene says.[13]

Any person, attacked by whatever passion, must oppose it diligently, as the Fathers teach. If we speak about carnal passion, anyone who is attacked by passion for a certain person must distance himself from him in every way. And this applies to conversation and close presence and the touch and even the smell of the clothing of the other person. If anyone does not observe all these cautions as he surrenders to such passion, he also fornicates in his heart, as the Fathers say, and he stokes the fiery furnace of lust as he allows such evil thoughts to enter as wild beasts.

2. Concerning Our Battles Against These Temptations of the Mind, Which Are to Be Conquered by the Remembrance of God's Presence and the Guarding of the Heart, That Is, by Prayer and Interior Silence. And Also Dealing with Spiritual Gifts.

The Fathers instruct us that our resistance against these temptations ought to be of equal strength to the force of the attack, whether we are to be victorious or to be defeated. This simply means that we should oppose such evil thoughts with as much strength as we can muster. By such struggle we will either gain the crown of life or the reward of torture: the crown to those victorious; the torture to those sinners who have not repented in this life.

Remembering God's Presence

Such sinfulness merits the reward of torture, says Peter Damascene, when in the concrete action a monk carries a tempting thought to its full completion. But those who battle strenuously and amidst a powerful battle against the enemy, they receive crowns of glory. The Fathers tell us also that a wise and outstanding way of battling these thoughts is to uproot them at the very beginning of the approaching thought, that is to say, at the assault of the thought as soon as it appears. They also teach us to pray unceasingly.

For by fighting against the first appearance of the thought, they tell us, we cut off all that would follow. Such a person who battles in so wise a manner turns away the mother of evil, namely, the wicked assault. And he ought to strive to make his mind deaf and speechless in prayer, as Nilus of Sinai says.[14] He holds his heart undisturbed from every thought, even if it be a good one. Hesychius of Jerusalem concurs with this advice.[15] For, after the dispassionate thoughts, he says, then the passionate ones follow, as our personal experience reveals, since it is the entrance of the former from which the guilt of the latter results.

And thus it is said that we must strive to hold our mind from even good thoughts, since evil thoughts come to us from them. For this reason we must continually silence our thoughts and look into the depths of our heart and say: "Lord, Jesus Christ, Son of God, have mercy on me," saying it fully. Sometimes we ought to say partially the words: "Lord, Jesus Christ, have mercy on me." And again change the words to: "Son of God, have mercy on me." Such a way of praying is more convenient for beginners, as Gregory of Sinai says.[16]

Praying the Jesus Prayer

However, he says that to change the wording of the prayer often is not advisable. The Fathers in our time add still another part of the prayer, as Gregory teaches: "Lord, Jesus Christ, Son of God, have mercy on me," and he then adds "a sinner." And this is good and most fitting for us sinners. Thus say the words with attention, while standing, sitting, or lying down. Take your mind and enclose it in your heart while you control your breathing by breathing as seldom as possible, as Symeon the New Theologian[17] and Gregory of Sinai teach. Call on the Lord Jesus with ardent desiring and patience as you resist all thoughts.

For the saints teach us to lengthen the breathing by not breathing too often, for this method is quite effective to bring the mind to a recollected state. However, if you cannot pray without thoughts in a silenced heart, but you find the thoughts multiplying, do not become discouraged, but remain in prayer. It is a well-known experience, as blessed Gregory of Sinai insists, that we who are laden by passions are aware that no beginner can control his mind and drive away thoughts that attack him unless God supports him and helps him to dispel such thoughts. It is the prerogative of the strong to hold the mind in check and drive away all thoughts, but even these do not turn away all thoughts by themselves, but they are supported in their struggles by God, who arms them with his grace and all his defenses.

If you see, Gregory says, the impurity of evil spirits in the thoughts that are presented in your mind, do not be frightened and do not wonder, even if such thoughts seem good to you. Do not give any attention to them, but control your breathing as much as you can and enclose your mind in your heart, as you arm yourself by calling on the Lord Jesus. Appeal to him, as often and consciously as possible, and the thoughts will dissolve as they are burnt up by the fiery, invisible rays radiating from your calling on the divine Name. But if such thoughts still greatly attack you, then stand up to pray against them and continue again with strength your original, ascetical work. How we should pray against the thoughts with God's help, we shall discuss later.

Pushing the Mind into the Heart: Prayer of the Heart

When you pray against them, if the thoughts still only assail you all the more and increase in number and you cannot keep your mind in your heart, then pray an oral prayer without ceasing, with strength and patience. If you find yourself becoming a bit slothful and fatigued, then call on God for help and force yourself to continue praying as best you can, never giving up on praying. Then all such thoughts will depart from you, as they are driven out by God's help. When you calm the mind from such phantasms, then enter into your heart and pray the prayer of the heart or the mind. For even though there are many good works, their value is only a partial good. The prayer of the heart is the source of all good and is likened to gardens that are refreshed by water, so does this prayer of the heart refresh the soul, as Gregory of Sinai teaches.

Blessed is the person who seriously meditates on the Writings of all the Spirit-filled Fathers and follows their teachings and examples. Such a person is completely taken up with this prayer and is able to overcome always every kind of thought, not only an evil one, but also one that seemingly is a good one. And in this manner, he attains perfect silence even in his thoughts, for the prayer is the peak and crown of all ascetical practices. For Symeon the New Theologian teaches that true silence and tranquillity (*hesychia*) is to seek the Lord in the heart, that is, to push the mind into the heart consciously and to pray and be concerned only with this.[18]

The attaining of this work, namely, the pushing of the mind down into the heart, which becomes freed of all thoughts, is difficult to accomplish, not only for beginners, but also for well-advanced persons in this work, if the latter have not yet received and maintained the sweetness of prayer in their hearts through the workings of grace. And we know from experience that for weak persons this work is very difficult and not very agreeable. However, when any person has obtained grace, then he prays without difficulty and lovingly, since he is comforted by grace. "And when the action of the prayer takes over," Gregory of Sinai says, "then truly the mind lives within the heart and brings joy and freedom to the person from all enslavement."

In regard to this work, if one should grow weary in prayer as he seeks to drive away all thoughts, let him relax by chanting a bit. Gregory says: "In patience remain seated, as the Apostle [Paul] says, 'Be long-suffering in prayer'" (Col 4:2). Do not be in a hurry to stop your praying, even if there is no sickening weakness or a lessening of the attacks of temptation urging you to cease. But while interiorly lamenting and weeping, remember the prophetic word: "As the pregnant mother approaches closer to the time of birth-giving, the greater becomes her suffering" (Jn 16:21). And as St. Ephrem also teaches the beginner: "Be sick over the sick state of your sicknesses, so that you may be delivered from all the vain sicknesses that afflict you." Gregory of Sinai likewise exhorts us that by inclining our head and neck, we should always patiently endure the time of prayer. We should sincerely call to the Lord Jesus for help, casting down the eyes and pushing the mind into the heart.

Let the words of our Lord himself be your support: "For the Kingdom of Heaven comes about by violence" (Mt 11:12). By these words the Lord means "having the utmost vigilance and suffering all kinds of toil." When the mind is worn down and weakened by toil and when the body and heart feel a certain sickness from the ardent and continued calling on the Lord Jesus, then change to chanting in order to give them a bit of respite and rest.

Persevering in Prayer

This, the Fathers say, is an excellent rule and teaching given by learned elders. And if a person is a solitary hermit or another has a disciple, they are advised to act thus. They say, that if one has a faithful disciple, let him read psalms as you meditate in your heart, not attending at all to the dreams and images which arise so you will not be seduced by them. Such dreamy fantasies occur when the mind rests in the heart and generates the prayer of the heart. The teachers tell us that only those perfected in the Holy Spirit, who have been set free by Jesus Christ, can control such fantasies.

One holy saint says that from his own experience we should concentrate all our efforts on saying the prayer [i.e., the Jesus Prayer] and reciting psalms only a little in order to dispel acedia[19] and to add a few penitential *tropars*,[20] but without any chanting, according to the teaching of John Climacus. And never chant in a sitting position, for St. Mark says: "The pangs of the heart born of piety will be their joy and the spiritual warmth will bestow on them joy and consolation." He teaches us always to recite the "Trisagion,"[21] and to add to all the chanting of Alleluias, according to the rule of the ancient Fathers Barsanuphius and Diadochus and others.

Mark teaches us also a rule to follow in accomplishing these exercises. He instructs us to pray for an hour, then to read for an hour, then to chant for an hour, and in this way we pass the day. He says this is a good procedure to follow, given the limits of time, means, and strength of each individual ascetic. Thus you can do as you like, either observe the suggestions given above or always practice the work of the Lord in complete recollection. But when your prayer is accompanied with sweetness of divine grace, and your prayer comes out of the depths of your heart, then it is recommended that you continue in that state.

Continue to Pray in Times of Consolation

If, therefore, you see that your prayer is operating unceasingly from the depths of your heart, and you are deeply centered, do not leave your prayer ever to rise and chant, lest your prayer will leave you, due to your negligence. For to leave God within you in order to seek him from outside is like leaving him from the heights to call on him by stooping lower. But when you allow any distraction to disturb the mind, such draws the mind away from silence. For silence is had only in peace and tranquillity, since God is peace and is beyond all agitation and noise.

But for those not skilled in such prayer, which is the source of all good works, and, according to John Climacus' teaching, waters the spiritual gardens of the soul, they should resort often to chanting and live according to different rule and canons. For hesychastic prayer of deep silence differs from the prayer of monks who live and observe the rule of the coenobitic life. There must be a proper balance in all things, according to the teachings of wise men. So there must be observed a proper measure for chanting as the Fathers have taught us. For those who are well advanced in prayer, it should be considered slothful to chant or read about the exploits of the lives of the Fathers.

No oars are needed if the sails of a boat are filled with wind to bring it across the sea of passion. But if the ship is standing still, then it is necessary to use oars or a rowboat to make progress. To those who seek to argue this point by quoting the holy Fathers, who speak of celebrating the all-night vigil service or uninterrupted chanting, Gregory of Sinai suggests to us this response from the writings of the Fathers: "Not all persons attain perfection in all things, due to human imperfections and a lack of zeal and physical strength. But what is small in the great saints is not totally small and what is great in the less perfect is not always perfect. For not all the ascetics in present or past times always traveled the same path or followed the same one to the end."

Concerning those who are progressing and who have reached a state of enlightenment, they are not required to recite psalms, but they are to practice silence, continued prayer, and contemplation, since they are living in union with God. They should not distract their mind from him nor permit it to be disturbed. For the minds of those who idly turn away from the remembrance of God and busy themselves with trivial matters, as St. Isaac teaches, commit spiritual adultery. He writes sublimely of such matters and insists on this: "When such persons possess such unspeakable joy, it cuts away any lip-prayer. Then the mouth and the tongue become silenced. Also the heart is silenced, which stands as a guard over fantasies along with the mind which directs the feeling senses and controls the thoughts that are like swift and bold flying birds."

Contemplative Prayer

"Then thinking no longer controls prayer, nor does it have any free movement or self-control. It no longer instructs, but it itself is instructed by a certain power which holds the reasoning power as a captive. It entertains ineffable matters and is not conscious of what it is." Isaac describes this as fearful reverence and contemplative prayer. He insists that the mind no longer prays with prayers, but has entered into the highest form of prayer, beyond any expression. For the mind no longer longs for any creature and, in the words of the Apostle Paul, does not know whether the person is in the body or out of the body (2 Cor 12:2). St. Isaac explains that prayer is like a seed and this ecstatic prayer is like the harvest. The harvesters are overwhelmed by the ineffable harvest they behold, that from such poor and naked seed such fruit should so quickly have sprung.

The Fathers call this "prayer," since this ineffable gift springs from prayer and is granted to the saints during prayer. As they cooperate, they enjoy such ecstasies and manifest spiritual thoughts, but no one knows its proper name. For whenever the soul is drawn by this spiritual activity, it is drawn to what is divine and becomes like to God by this unapproachable union. The soul is illumined in its movements by a ray of light from on high. And when the mind is able to have a foretaste of the beatific vision to come, then it forgets itself and all earthly creatures and is not at all attracted to anything else. And it is said elsewhere that in time of prayer the mind is raised up beyond any desire as it enters into the realm of incorporeal thoughts, which are not within the experience of the senses. In a flash you are enraptured with joy. The tongue is paralyzed by silence as the soul feasts on this ineffable food. A certain joyful sweetness flows out from the heart, while a person is drawn away by this delight from all sensate creatures. His whole body is overcome by such nourishment and joy, such as the natural tongue is unable to describe.

Ineffable Joy

Even all that is of this earth seems to be like ashes and dung. It is taught that, when such sweetness overcomes a person, overcoming his whole being, at that time he thinks he is in nothing less than the Kingdom of Heaven. And in another place, it is said that one who has found this joy in God is no longer aware of any passionate movement, but he even forgets his very own life because the love of God is sweeter than life. And the wisdom of God is sweeter than honey and the honeycomb and from it love is born.

But this is ineffable and one is unable to communicate it in human words, as Symeon the New Theologian says: "What tongue can ever describe it? What mind can ever speak of it? What homily can express it? This is so awesome, truly awesome! and beyond any words. I behold a light, which the world cannot contain, glowing in the middle of my cell as I sit on my bed. Within my very own being I contemplate the Maker of the world and I converse with him and love him and feed on him. I am nourished only by this beautiful, divine vision, and I unite myself with him as I rise upward above the heavens. Only this one thing I know and it is the truth. But where my body is then I do not know." And conversing further about the Lord, Symeon says: "He indeed loves me and takes me to himself and hides me in his embrace, even though he is in Heaven. Yet he is also in my heart. And I look upon him, both here and there." And further Symeon speaks to the Lord: "Master, this shows me to be equal to the angels and even superior to them for your essence is not visible to them and your being is unapproachable to them. Yet you are entirely visible to me and your substance is united with my being."

It is this that St. Paul writes of when he declares: "Eye has not seen, nor ear heard, nor have entered into the heart of man the things which God has prepared for those who love him" (1 Cor 2:9). St. Symeon continues: "In this state I have no desire to leave my cell, but rather I wish only to hide deeply as in a pit in the earth and there, removed from the entire world, I would gaze upon my immortal Master and Creator."

St. Isaac also agrees with this description as he writes: "When the blinders of the passions are lifted from the eyes of the mind and a person contemplates this glory, then he is elevated aloft and covered with awe. And if God did not put a limit to such experiences in his earthly existence, how long would a person not wish to dwell always in it? And if such an experience were allowed to endure throughout a person's earthly life, he would never wish to depart from this wonderful vision."

But God out of his mercy lessens his grace for a time in his saints so as to allow them, through their preaching of the word and their example, to serve the brethren, as St. Macarius says of those who have advanced in perfection: "The love and sweetness of such amazing visions are like a mighty flaming fire. And if, it is taught, a person entertained such a grace at all times, he would not be able to hear or speak with other earthly beings or have any concern with weaker persons. He would have arrived at the peak of the twelfth degree of perfection. But, it is said, this grace diminishes and he takes one step down to the eleventh degree."[22] To such the full measure of perfection will not be given so that they may have time to exercise themselves on behalf of the brethren in contemplative service in actions.

But what shall we say about those who, being still in this mortal existence, yet have been nourished by immortal food and have been deemed capable of receiving even in this passing world a part of the joys that will await us in the heavenly fatherland? Such as these no longer pine after the beautiful and sweet pleasures of this world, nor are they frightened by life's sorrows and evil sufferings. With the Apostle [Paul] they have the strength to say: "What can ever separate us from the love of God?" (Rom 8:39).

All this, according to the teaching of St. Isaac, pertains to those who have seen such visions and have felt them in their very own being. They have obtained this gift through the guidance of the Fathers and in imitating their zealous exploits and labors in their own lives. But we, so burdened and guilty of many sins and preyed upon by many passions, are not worthy even to hear about such topics. However, by relying upon God's grace, we can dare at least to speak about these things found in the words of the Spirit-filled Fathers, so that we can acknowledge, even though never fully, the degree of degradation into which we have fallen.

We can at least be conscious of the folly that engrosses us, of how we throw away our talents in the pursuit of material things as we give ourselves over to cares and anxieties that are harmful for our souls. And we regard all such pursuit as good and praiseworthy! But woe to us! We do not understand the worth of our souls. We do not understand that we have not been called to live such an evil life, as St. Isaac says. Woe to us if we think our life in this world—its sufferings, its joys, its rest—has importance for us! Woe to us if by the life of our soul, so weighed down by laziness, worldly curiosity, and lack of concern, we should be convinced that the style of life that was proper to that lived by the ancient saints is no longer necessary for us nor is it possible for us to live such ascetical exploits. No, this cannot be so, in no way! Such practices are not possible only for those who are immersed by self-indulging passions because of their own free will who do not seriously desire to repent, namely, to truly come under the guidance of the divine Holy Spirit, but who are given over to useless, worldly cares.

Guarding the Heart

But for those who sincerely seek to repent, and who seek God in love and fear, and have him alone before their eyes and walk according to his commandments, God will accept all of them, granting his mercy and giving them his grace and glorifying them. Thus all of Holy Scripture assures us of this.

In ancient times many Fathers themselves walked in this exemplary way of life and directed others accordingly. But now it is not the same, due to a great lack of such spiritual directors. But whoever dedicates himself completely to the work of God, God's very own grace will wisely guide him, being his strength now and for all ages, in the life to come. But to those who do not desire to undertake the ascetical life and are full of vanity, even in our present time God does not give his gift as he did to the saints of old. Such persons the Apostle [Paul] calls the seduced ones who lead others astray. Persons such as these do not with to listen to the fact that God's grace is always in this moment available. Gregory of Sinai calls them the utmost blinded, nonfeeling, unwise persons, lacking in faith. We, discerning from the holy Writings, if we wish diligently to be occupied with the divine world, should distance ourselves as far as possible from the vanities of this world. Let us be engaged in uprooting the passions, keeping our heart from any evil thoughts and fulfilling in general all God's commandments.

In order to guard the heart, it is necessary to pray unceasingly. In this consists the first stage of a monk's development and without which it is impossible to put to death the passions, as Symeon the New Theologian says.

Praying at Night

The best, most graceful time for a monk's spiritual exercises is at night. As the holy Fathers said: "It is during nighttime that the monk must best be engaged in his work." Blessed Philotheus of Sinai teaches that the mind is purified best at night. And St. Isaac says: "Consider every prayer which we offer up in the night to be more important than all our daily actions. For the sweet consolation which the one who fasts receives during the day comes out of the light received during the monk's nocturnal exercises." Other saints are in accord with this teaching. For this reason, St. John Climacus teaches: "At night be occupied much more with prayer than with chanting." In another place he says: "But if you grow weary from mental prayer, get up and pray on your feet."

In this manner we ought to conduct ourselves when the mind becomes heavy from mental prayer, that is, let the monk occupy himself with chanting psalms or *tropars* or something else, as long as it is enjoined by one's rule. But in this matter we must remember that "many words," according to the teachings of John Climacus, "often distract the mind during the time of prayer while few words often gather the mind to a focus." "When we are attacked by phantasms," as St. Isaac teaches, "we would do better to occupy ourselves with some reading." Thus also did the angel teach St. Anthony the Great: "When your mind becomes scattered, then it is better to turn to reading or manual labor."[23] For the novices, when they find themselves assailed by temptations, it is very helpful to do some kind of manual work along with prayer or service in the occupations given by obedience, especially and more importantly, those tasks required of them in order to arm themselves against temptations of depression and acedia,[24] as the Fathers teach us.

Guarding the Thoughts

In general in this matter of guarding the thoughts, St. Hesychius of Jerusalem offers us four ways: (1) to guard the thoughts at their first manifestation, that is to say, to follow or observe them and resist them at the very beginning; (2) to hold the heart silent at its deepest center where it is free from all phantasms; (3) to call upon the Lord Jesus Christ for help; (4) to have before you the remembrance of your own death. All these ways close the doors to evil thoughts. And each of these methods, whichever one you may choose, this is called *nepsis*,[25] or sober vigilance of our mind, in a word, known simply as "mental activity." Paying attention to all of these ways, each of us should undertake the battle according to what is the best way for himself.

3. By What Means We May Gain Strength to Resist the Attacks of Evil Thoughts.

One way to strengthen oneself in the inner battle and the struggle against temptations, described in all the Writings, consists in this, that when we will be attacked by evil thoughts, we will not be disheartened, nor become depressed, nor give up nor discontinue the longer course itself on the road of the ascetical life. When we are bitterly assailed by sordid temptations, the cunningness of the devil instills in us the false feeling of shame so that we will be hindered from turning our eyes to God in heartfelt repentance and petitioning for strength to turn against such thoughts. But let us conquer these thoughts by constant repentance and unceasing prayer, and not surrender our arms to our enemies, that is, let us not turn back, even though each day we receive from them a thousand wounds. Let us firmly determine never to give up this life-giving activity, even until the moment of our death. For along with such temptations, we receive also a secret visitation of God's mercy.

St. Isaac teaches that it is not only ourselves who are full of passion and weakness and are subject to defeats in the mental battle. There are also those who have already reached a high degree of purity who lead under God's protective wisdom outstanding lives in blessed silence and after all this peace and consolation and chaste and gentle thoughts, they also are tempted. Oh, how much more, then, should a person who is so weak and powerless be wounded and overthrown to the ground from his helplessness? But one day when he will snatch the banner from the hands of his powerful enemy, then his name will be praised before all. He will be lifted up among those who excelled in battle and he will receive the crown of victory and other precious spiritual gifts. His reward will be greater than that of his companions.

See how the saints encourage us and remove far from our mind all doubt so that we may not weaken in the battle against evil thoughts or become victims of despair.

Ways to Cultivate Inner Attentiveness

But when you are deemed worthy of the presence of God's gift of grace, you should not become careless, that is, you should not give in to complacency nor become puffed up. Rather, you should turn humbly to God and give thanks to him and remember your sins, which you have committed by his permission. Recall how you have fallen so low then and how animal-like was your unthinking mind. Meditate on the depraved condition of your nature. Ponder upon the impure thoughts and disgusting fruits which gripped your soul when it was frozen without the warmth of God's grace. Imagine that time of torturous and disordered movement which overtook you, not so very long ago when you lay in such blindness. Recall how quickly and suddenly you bowed down before your passions as you took delight in them only to heap more burdens upon yourself in the darkened state of your mind. And remember all of this as you weep and reproach yourself.

Consider this, that God's divine providence brings all this upon us in order that we may be humbled. See what blessed Gregory of Sinai teaches about this purpose: "Until a person will have experienced having been utterly defeated and conquered, until he has been deeply wounded by every kind of passion and temptation, even if he does not receive evil wounds inflicted upon his soul as he does not find any help in the actions he performs nor any help from God or from any other creature, so that he is driven to the condition of despair, only then can he have true repentance and be humbled to consider himself lower than all others, since he regards himself as the least slave before all others and the worst of even the devils themselves. Only then can he realize that he was beset and conquered by them."

And so divine providence arranges this for the purpose of instructing a person in humility. After such an experience there always follows a second and greater gift from God. God elevates the individual by giving to the humbled person the divine power to act and accomplish in him all things, even to perform miracles as he realizes he is God's instrument.

Pay attention to this with fear. If you are not humble in your wisdom, grace will leave you and you naturally will be defeated by your being tempted by ordinary daily temptations. For you are unable to stand steadfast in virtue by your own power. This is the work of grace which upholds you as a mother carries her child in her arms. God's grace protects you from all adversity. We must pay great attention to this, so that we will not be guilty but will actually be strengthened by the occasion of evil thoughts. Otherwise, this happens in such circumstances when we journey on the divine path, and we do not progress rightly, not sincerely and not steadily. Thus, whoever wishes to strive for perfection in God's love, who truly seeks to be saved and strives to do God's work, such a person should live in his cell with great zeal and attention and, as much as his strength allows, let him live the ascetical life in all details in accord with the holy Writings, fulfilling all with piety in humility and always with zeal, without any laziness and weakening.

4. GUIDELINES TO ALL ACTIVITIES IN OUR SKETE-LIFE.

The fulfilling of all the activities in our skete-life consists in this, namely, that we must always in all our activities seek to do all in soul and body, in word or deed and thought, as far as our strength allows, to do all godly activities with God and in God.

Blessed Philotheus teaches that just as when we were still living in the world, surrounded by its illusions, we strongly were bent with all our mind and our feelings to enjoy sinful attractions, so it should be fitting now, since we have begun to live the skete common monastic life, to live for God. With all our mind and all our feelings we ought to work for the glory of the living and true God by aligning ourselves with his truth and will. We should fulfill all his holy commandments and drive away anything to the contrary in every activity that would be unpleasing to God according to the word of God: "I rule myself by all your precepts; I hate all deceptive paths" (Ps 119:128).

In particular, when we rise from sleep, before all else it is imperative to praise God aloud and confess to him and then begin our spiritual activities, that is, our prayer, chanting, reading, manual work, and whatever else we must do, whatever makes up our lesser important tasks. The mind must always be focused positively on God with deep reverence, devotion, and trust in order to do all unto God's good pleasure and not out of vainglory or to please other human beings. For we should be solidly convinced that he "who is everywhere and fills all things," the Lord, is with us. For he who gave us our ears hears all and who created our eyes sees all.

If you converse with someone, let your conversation be pleasing to God. Keep from complaining, from judging others, from idle words and quarreling. In such a way also conduct yourself as you eat and drink, by doing all in the fear and reverence of God. Especially we ought to be piously recollected and let our limbs recline at night in decency. For our present sleep is an image of our eternal sleep, that is, our death and our lying on our couch should remind us of our lying in the grave. And in all things we must always have God before our eyes according to the example of David, who speaks of himself: "I keep Yahweh before me always for with him at my right hand, nothing can shake me" (Ps 16:8). If we conduct ourselves in this manner we will pray unceasingly.

Whoever is healthy in body, let him mortify himself by fasting, observing vigils, and performing acts that demand strength and bring him fatigue. For example, our prostrations and hard manual works should be done so that the body will be conquered by the soul and we may be delivered from the passions by the grace of Christ.[26]

But if one's body is weak, it should be dealt with according to its weakness. Concerning prayer, let no one neglect it, neither the healthy nor the weak persons. For bodily labor in the required measure is demanded of those who are endowed with a healthy and strong body. In regard to the work of controlling the thoughts, it consists of entertaining the mind with godly thoughts and to remember the presence of God in order to center oneself powerfully upon the love of God. This work is of obligation upon all without any exception, not even exempting those lying in bed with a serious sickness.

In regard to our relations with our neighbors, according to God's commandments we must always show love. Toward those who live near to us, let us show our love in word and deed insofar as it never violates our love for God. And toward those who are far away from us, we should stretch out spiritually our love toward them as we drive away from our hearts every kind of evil opinion of them. We should bow our souls reverently before them and fulfill the desire to serve them sincerely. If the Lord sees us acting thus, he will forgive us our sins and he will accept our prayers as a worthy sacrifice, and shower upon us his mercies.

A Summary of What Was Written Above

Thus we have briefly explained by God's grace, from the holy Writings, concerning the mental activity, that is to say the various adverse obstacles and the struggles which occur in undergoing such asceticism. We dealt with what counterattacks on our part are necessary, that is, what is the best manner for engaging in this warfare, namely, to maintain one's heart in prayer without any thoughts. Having explained at length the strength needed and how to accomplish all this, I pointed out the holy teachings on this subject and how with God's grace I am able actually to journey on this road, even though I am unworthy to touch on such matters. Still, I taught about how those laborers in such a great undertaking can be strengthened and about how to live such a life. I also dealt with anyone desiring earnestly to attain the first and most important battle: the great victory, that is, a still-pointed mind and authentic prayer. Now after that, with God's permission, let me teach also about other various ways of engaging in the battles and how to attain victory.

5. Concerning Various Ways of Doing Battle Against and Gaining Victory Over the Eight Fundamental Temptations of the Flesh and Other Temptations.

The Fathers teach us that there are various ways of fighting evil temptations in thoughts and different ways of defeating them, depending on the measure and degrees of perfection already attained in the ascetical life, namely, by praying against such thoughts or by entering into the battle against them or by turning them away by contemning them. To show contempt is to suppress and drive out such thoughts and is only for the most perfect. To resist them by contending against them head on is for those intermediate ones who are making progress. For new beginners and the weaker ones, they should pray and turn the evil thoughts away by evoking good ones, as St. Isaac enjoins upon us: "Under the guise of good virtues passions are conquered." Or as Peter Damascene teaches: "To repel bad thoughts hasten with a good thought." And so also have other Fathers taught.

And also when temptations assail us like a sudden storm so that we do not find ourselves in a state of peace and inner stillness to pray properly, then it is fitting to pray about the very tempting thoughts and thus turn the evil ones to beneficial ones. And how we should pray about this or that thought and how to change an evil one into something good I will present from the holy Writings.

The Eight Principal Vices of the Soul

The holy Fathers taught that there are eight principal vices of the soul from which numerous other temptations are the offspring. These are (1) gluttony, (2) fornication, (3) covetousness, (4) anger, (5) sadness, (6) acedia, (7) vainglory, (8) pride.[27] And so the Fathers place as first gluttony so we also will speak of it first, so that we may not unwisely change the order of the very wise Fathers. Let us do likewise by following the teachings of the holy Fathers.

a. GLUTTONY

If you are attacked, that is, a strong and alluring enticement of gluttony tempts you, presenting you with thoughts of various delicious and appetizing foods and drinks along with the temptation to overindulge yourself in more than you need and to eat at the improper times, call to mind then first of all the words of the Lord: "Watch yourselves or your hearts will be given over to debauchery and drunkenness" (Lk 21:34). Pray to him and call to him for help as you reflect on what the Fathers taught: "The basic passion in monks and root of all evil and especially of fornication is gluttony."

And in the very beginning of human history the crime of our forefather Adam from which all else flowed was the vice of gluttony, for he tasted the forbidden food and lost paradise. And all his posterity underwent death, as it is said somewhere: "In beholding the beautiful and good food, it became for me a death-dealing fruit." From that time until now many have been enslaved by gluttony. In times past and in our present time many fall with a great fall as is known in the holy Writings and from experience.[28]

Another help to avoid gluttony is to ponder, as Barsanuphius the Great teaches,[29] on the fleetingness of delicate and delicious foods, how quickly they decompose and shortly there is nothing left. Thus overcome the passion or vice of gluttony by using food and drink in the proper measure and at the proper time.

1. Measure of Food

In regard to the daily measure and quantity of food to be eaten, the Fathers have taught that each person should freely determine for himself in the following way: If a monk seems to feel an excessive fullness after a meal, let him decrease the amount during the next meal. But when he sees that the amount of food he had taken was inadequate to sustain his bodily energy, let him then increase the amount a bit more. And in this way after he has learned what is necessary through experience, he should settle upon such a quantity of food that can support his bodily strength. Thus he will not be a slave to the pleasure of the palate, but be guided by what is truly necessary.

Thus in this way whatever will be placed before him, let him eat it, giving thanks to God as he judges himself as unworthy of the food. It is, therefore, impossible to give for all persons only one measure of food, because there are various bodies with differing strength and power, just as copper, iron, and wax differ from each other. In general a novice can be guided by the best rule, namely to stop eating food when he feels still a bit hungry. But if he feels full, he does not sin in this. But having allowed himself to eat to satiety, let him reproach himself. In this manner he will transform the attack of his enemy and put himself on the path to victory over the enemy.

2. Time for Eating

The Fathers enjoin upon us fasting, that is, not to take any food until the ninth hour.[30] But whoever wishes to fast longer from food, let him freely do so. In general, the Fathers have suggested the following. During spring and fall we should take food when the day begins to decline, which is after two hours beyond noon, the "ninth hour" or according to our reckoning about three o'clock in the afternoon in spring. But in our northern clime in summer and winter, both for the days and the nights, the hours of sunrise and sunset differ from those countries around the Mediterranean, in Palestine, or in the city of Constantinople. For this reason we should fast depending on the length of the days, whether shorter or longer. On a day when no fasting is prescribed, we can begin a bit earlier the time of the main meal and if necessary also to eat a small collation in the evening.

3. Different Foods

In regard to the different kinds of foods, we should take a little of all that is offered us, including sweets. Gregory of Sinai gives this as a wise rule: "Never pick and choose or refuse to eat any of the food offered, but let the monks give to God thanks for everything and thus keep their souls from any self-exaltation." In this way, fleeing from any pride, we will drive far from us any disdain toward the good God's beautiful creation. Still, it is useful for those who are weak in faith or virtue to abstain from certain meats, especially from the more pleasing to the taste, because they do not have the adequate confidence and trust in God's Providence that they will be able to eat them without spiritual harm. For them the Apostle [Paul] enjoins: "One man can in conscience eat whatever he wills, while another who is scrupulous must be content with vegetables" (Rom 14:2).

When any food is found harmful to anybody because either of one's sickly condition or bodily complications, let him not force himself to eat what is harmful, but let him eat what is good for him. For Basil the Great teaches: "It is not proper to fight against the body with food which should rather serve to preserve in health the body."[31] (St. Basil, *Long Rule; PG* 31: 969A.)

4. Various Types of Bodies

Whoever has a healthy and strong body should work himself strenuously, as much as he is able to do. May we thus deliver ourselves from vices and let the body by Christ's grace be humbly submissive to the soul. But whoever has a weak and sickly body let him give to his body rest so that he may not fall in the end. For those who are underweight, let them not overeat, but give to the body whatever it needs by way of food and drink. In the time of war one must manfully withstand bodily the enemy. How many, not controlling their appetite, fall into a ditch of the vice of impurity and sordidness not describable in words. But when there is good order and discipline in the matter of gluttony, every kind of virtue is also in evidence. As the great Basil says: "If you withstand gluttony you will enter into paradise. But if you do not discipline yourself in this matter, you gain only the prize of death, eternal death."

Because of any difficulty in making a journey or from any other taxing work, a person should give his body some indulgences. He should give the body a bit more beyond the usual amount in food and drink and in sleep. And for this he should not merit any judgment from others nor should others consider this disgraceful since he has acted with prudence and discretion.

b. FORNICATION

Great is the struggle by which we must contend in the matter of fornication, which is in a special way a fierce and painful battle since it is fought in the soul as well as on the body level.[32] Therefore, we must strive powerfully and constantly to keep with courage and diligence one's heart free from thoughts of fornication. This is especially true when the holy community gathers to receive the holy Eucharist. For it is then especially that the enemy tries every stratagem to soil our conscience.

And when these sensuous temptations attack you, then fill yourself with the fear of God. Recall that nothing can be hidden from God, not even the most delicate movements of the heart. The Lord is judge and sees all, even the most hidden. And he will be our judge and prosecutor. We then must also keep before our mind our vow which we have professed before angels and men, a vow to live in chastity and purity. Chastity and purity are lived out, not only in our exterior, but also in the deepest reaches of our heart, for it is there that the heart is set free from impure thoughts and becomes most honorable and pleasing before God. But anyone who often gives himself over to such sensuous thoughts of fornication and sullies himself by these commits fornication in his heart, as the Fathers taught. And if one does not guard himself from such thoughts, he is led to act them out. And what a great pity! The evil of such an act is seen in this, namely, that no other sin is seen as so evil by the Fathers, who call it the "fall," since a person who has fallen into this sin is without hope and is thrown into despair.

During the struggle against fornication it is helpful for us, I think, to carefully reflect on our ideal and the monastic calling in which we find ourselves. Consider carefully that we have been clothed in the habit of the angels.[33] How can we spoil our conscience and destroy the angelic-like image by impure lust? Let us call to mind what shame and scandalous example we give to other human beings. For by such thoughts of shame and scandal we can resist such shameful, unworthy thoughts. Ought we not really to wish to die rather than to be accused of such a shameful condition? By this and other means let us strive to cut off such impure thoughts.

1. Unceasing Prayer for Victory in this Matter
The main and powerful and victory-granting means to combat such an impure spirit consists in unceasing prayer to the Lord God, as the holy Fathers teach. St. Maximus the Confessor instructs us to arm ourselves against lustful thoughts by prayer, using the words for prayer of the psalmist David: "The enemy surrounds me now" (Ps 17:11), and "My Joy, thou art my refuge when the enemy besieges me" (Ps 32:7). John Climacus speaks similarly: "O God, come to my assistance!" (Ps 61:1), and similar quotes. He bears witness concerning the need to pray earnestly against such temptations to those saints who were especially noted for their ascetical practices and labors in preserving their purity and chastity. For example, Daniel the Solitary enjoined upon a brother-monk, greatly struggling against fornication, to pray and call for help to the martyr Thomaida, who was killed for her chastity, by praying: "O God, by the prayer of your martyr Thomaida, help me!" And the struggling brother at once was delivered from the vice of fornication. Keeping in mind such witnesses, let us pray and call for help upon those mentioned in the holy Writings as having struggled with chastity and purity.

2. A Desperate Cry unto the Lord
When the struggle is especially violent, then we should rise to our feet and, lifting our eyes and our arms heavenward, pray as the great Gregory of Sinai teaches and God will drive away such thoughts. Pray in the way St. Isaac taught us: "You are mighty, Lord, and this is your battle. You do wage it and gain the victory

for us."[34] And so John Climacus teaches: "Cry out aloud to the All-Mighty to save you, not by clever words, but by humble and simple speech: 'Have mercy on me, O Lord, for I am weak!'" And you will experience the power of the All-High and you will drive away your invisible enemies. Always beat your enemies back by the name of Jesus. For you will find in heaven and on earth no more powerful means than this.

John Climacus notes that the devil chases after us and at the very time when he notices that we cannot arm ourselves against him, which should be both external and internal, then he especially attacks us. Take warning and do not weaken in prayer, especially at such time when evil thoughts torment you. Guard your bodily and spiritual eyes as will be best for you at the time and according to your strength.

And if you will do such, you will know from experience that by the power of the All-High and his invisible help such thoughts will mightily be conquered. But if you are lazy, then you will be put to shame. How conquered you will be by those temptations and overwhelmed by an evil conscience! We must realize that this diabolical cunningness, as the Fathers have taught, by which the devil lodges in our mind such thoughts, especially calling to mind the fair faces of women and young boys, must be resisted at once even if they should be the countenances of pious persons. What passions can evidently arise from such thoughts? But if you delay resisting them, the evil tempter conveniently twists and clothes such thoughts into sordid and abominable images. It happens at times that we ourselves can be filled with remorse by such lustful thoughts. We should examine ourselves about them. We catch ourselves in these thoughts, wishing such filth even while we are tormented by them. Such desires reduce us to our basic, unnatural lust, similar to that of animals, even though they do not uncommonly lust.

3. Cautions To Be Heeded

For those very sensate persons, especially novices, they must guard themselves against such examinations lest they linger excessively upon such thoughts, thinking that they are fighting against them whereas they may be really yielding to the vice. For this reason it is best that we resist the first presentation, the very beginning of such temptations. To wage war against these is possible only for those strong persons who have acquired the habit of drawing good from reflections on such thoughts.

Finally, you must avoid any conversations with women, and even looking at them. Keep away from living with youths with effeminate and pretty faces and refrain from looking at them. For this is a device of the devil to tempt monks, as someone of the Fathers has taught. And if it is necessary, do not be alone with them, says St. Basil, in any unnecessary case, for nothing is more important to you than your soul, for which Christ has died and has risen. And we should not desire even to listen to anybody in any improper conversations which may stir up any such passions.

c. COVETOUSNESS

The sickness of covetousness, as the Fathers teach us,[35] comes from outside of our own nature and is the result of a lack of faith and intelligence. For this reason it can be resisted without much difficulty by those who stand attentive with the fear of God and who genuinely wish to be saved. But if this disease becomes rooted in us, it becomes the most evil of all other vices. And if we succumb to it, it brings us to a great perdition. The Apostle [Paul] called it not only the root of all evil, that is, anger, sadness, and the other vices, but it is in itself an idolatry (1 Tm 6:10; Col 3:5).

Because of covetousness, many have not only fallen from a pious life, but, sinning in the matter of faith, came to perdition in soul and body, as it is taught in the holy Writings. And the Fathers taught that "the person who gathers gold and silver and places his trust in them no longer believes in the truth that God will provide for him." And also the holy Writings teach that if anyone is led captive by pride or covetousness, the devil needs no other weapon against him, for one or the other of these vices will sufficiently bring about that person's destruction. Therefore, it behooves us to keep ourselves from all destructive and psychosomatic vices and to pray to the Lord God that he may cut out of us any spirit of covetousness. We must drive from ourselves not only any desire for gold, silver, and property, but also for all other creatures except what are needed for our use as clothing, shoes, a cell, dishes, and tools for manual labor. And all such as these should be cheap, unadorned, and easily obtainable. Nor should these be the cause for any cares and preoccupations and worries so that we do not fall into contact with the spirit of the world. True victory over covetousness and the temptation to be attached to material creatures comes not only when we do not have anything, but when we do not even wish to possess anything. This gives us spiritual purity.

d. ANGER

If the temptation of anger assails us, it means we are forced to recall the wrongs done to us and are moved to a rage in order to seek revenge for the evil done to us. At such times we must remember the words of the Lord: "If brother does not forgive his brother with all his heart, then your heavenly Father will not pardon your sins" (Mt 18:35; Mk 11:26). And likewise everyone who wishes to receive pardon of his sins must first forgive from the heart his brother. For the Lord has commanded us to ask pardon of our debts just as we forgive others. It is clear that, if we ourselves do not forgive, then we will not be forgiven (Mt 6:12, 15). Moreover, we must also understand that even if we think we are acting rightly, but we do not give up our anger, this is offensive to God.

The Fathers have taught: "If an angry person were to raise a dead person, his prayer would not be acceptable to God." The Fathers do not mean by this teaching that an angry man could really restore life to a dead person, but only to stress how dead is such a prayer before God.[36] For this reason we ought never to become angry nor do any evil to a brother monk, not only in deed nor in word, but also in a look, for such a person by one glance can insult his brother, as the Fathers have taught. Angry thoughts flow out of the heart. We gain a great victory over such thoughts of anger when we pray for the brother insulting us, as Abbas Dorotheus enjoins upon us in these words: "Help, O Lord, my brother, and on account of his prayers, have mercy on me, a sinner."[37] Such a prayer for a brother is love and compassion, but to call on the help of his prayer is humility. And thus we fulfill the law of Christ: "Love your enemies, do good to those who hate you, pray for those who persecute and insult you" (Mt 5:44).

To him who fulfills this command, the Lord has promised a reward above all others. He promised not only the heavenly Kingdom and not only consolation and joy among other rewards, but the very sonship. As the Lord said: "You will be sons of your Father, who is in Heaven" (Mt 5:45). The Lord himself, having given us this commandment, teaches us by his example in order that we might imitate him according to our strength. How much evil did he endure for the sake of us sinners and still he did not show anger to those evil persecutors, but he prayed on their behalf to his Father: "Father, forgive them their sin" (Lk 23:34). And so also all the saints, following his path, received grace. For they not only did not return evil to those who persecuted them, but they also prayed for them, covering over their failings. They rejoiced when they reformed themselves. They treated them always with mercy and love.

e. SADNESS

It is no small feat to struggle against the spirit of sadness, for it can drive our spirit into perdition and despair. If any suffering inflicted upon us from people should be borne with greater generosity of spirit by us, the motive for this should be to pray powerfully (as we said earlier), seeing that all things that befall us are not contrary to divine Providence. For everything sent to us is sent by God. He sends such always for our profit and the salvation of our souls.

And if what is sent to us does not seem to us at the time helpful, it will later be seen clearly to have been truly beneficial for us, not as we ourselves wish, but as God arranges. We should, therefore, not exaggerate with our human ideas these hardships, but we should believe with all our heart that the eye of God sees all and that nothing can happen to us without his will. He sends us temptations according to his goodness, that, bearing them, we can receive his crown. Without temptations no one can ever receive the crown. Therefore, being in the throes of temptations, we should give thanks to God, our Benefactor and Savior, for these. As St. Isaac teaches:

"Lips that give thanks always are worthy to be blessed by God and such a grateful heart walks in grace." (38)

We ought to refrain from any kind of complaining against those who persecute us. For the holy Father himself says that God bears with all the failings of human beings, but he will punish him who always complains. But it is necessary to mourn over our sins, since this is beneficial to us for repentance, but only if accompanied with hope and trust in God. This is based on the truth that there is no sin which exceeds the mercy of God which he will not forgive totally to those who are truly repentant and pray. Such sadness is accompanied with joy. It makes a sincere monk open to receive all that is good and gives him strength to bear all sorts of misfortunes with patience. As the Apostle [Paul] taught: "Supernatural remorse leads us to an abiding and salutary change of heart, whereas the world's remorse leads to death" (2 Cor 7:10).

But this other kind of sadness, a remorse inspired by devils, must be driven out from our heart, just as all other vices are driven out by prayer and spiritual reading, by contact and conversation with people leading a spiritual life.[38] For sadness which is not of God becomes the root of all evil. And if such sadness stays with us for a long time, it soon takes the form of despair. It renders the soul empty and dry without any strength and patience and the monk becomes slothful in prayer and spiritual reading.

f. ACEDIA

If acedia conquers us, a great battle must be fought with all one's strength. This cruel and oppressive spirit of acedia is accompanied with the spirit of sadness or follows after it. It is especially oppressive and a heavy burden for monks, who live the solitary, silent life.

When the cruel waves of acedia rise up, the monk loses hope of ever seeing an end to them, but the enemy suggests concerning this spirit of acedia the defeating thought to the monk that as great as is his suffering at the present time, what will follow in the coming days will increase even more intensely in suffering. He will be tempted, thinking that he has been deserted by God, that God has no longer any care over him, that this has happened to him outside of any divine providence and that only to him alone has such suffering befallen and that others never suffered or are suffering as he does. But no, this is not so! God, as a Father, loving his children, inflicts this not only upon us sinners, but also on his saints, who down through the ages have been pleasing to him. He beats them with this spiritual rod out of his love for his very own children in order that they may make progress in virtues.

But such a heavy state of the spirit quickly and unfailingly changes. And such a state is followed by a visitation of divine mercy and consolation. Just in one evil-embattled hour the monk does not think that he can further continue persevering in living the upright ascetical life. The enemy tempts him to turn away from all the good he has already done. But now almost in a second all turns for him, bathing him in light. All is done now easily. All sadness disappears as though it never existed. The monk again finds himself zealously applying himself to the life of virtue and he is amazed at the change for the better that he now finds in himself. Now his resolution to live a holy and God-pleasing life becomes more determined. He understands that God in his mercy arranges all things for his benefit and a temptation happens solely out of God's love for him for his perfection.

1. How to Cope with Acedia

And so the monk is more enflamed with love for God as he acknowledges without a doubt that "God is faithful and never tempts us beyond our strength" (1 Cor 10:13). Without God's permission the enemy can do nothing against us. The devil saddens our spirit only to the degree that God grants him his permission. Now the monk, knowing this from his own experiences, grows in greater and greater wisdom through the changes that have taken place in his spirit. He now valiantly bears every kind of suffering that comes to him, knowing full well that there is nothing that can prevent him from proving his love for God as he bears with great generosity all sufferings that come to him.

He realizes that this suffering leads him to higher perfection. John Climacus has taught this: "Nothing can so prepare a monk for the crown as much as acedia if only he pushes himself without any faltering to perform his spiritual exercises." When the struggle becomes terrifying against the spirit of acedia, then one should protect himself from the spirit of ingratitude and not fall into the danger of blasphemy. For the enemy in the time of acedia powerfully attacks the soul by these means, namely, by the weapons of blasphemy and ingratitude.

A monk, vanquished by acedia, becomes full of doubt, fear, and despair by the suggestion of the enemy that he cannot obtain God's mercy and be forgiven his sins, nor be delivered from eternal punishment of hell and obtain heaven. And many other evil temptations then join to assail his soul in ways too terrifying, beyond any description. Such thoughts do not cease to assail the soul at any time, whether the monk is engaged in spiritual reading or chanting the Office. The ascetic must then use all his strength in order not to succumb to despair and not give up praying. As much as one's strength allows, the monk should then pray, and in such prayer it is very helpful to prostrate oneself face down.

2. How to Pray in Times of Acedia

Let the monk, filled with acedia, pray as Barsanuphius instructs us: "Lord, look upon my suffering and be merciful to me, a sinner!" Or according to the teaching of Symeon the New Theologian pray in this way: "Do not permit any temptation or suffering or sickness to befall me, O Lord, that would be beyond my strength. But deliver me from them and grant me strength to bear them even with gratitude." At times it is good to pray against such vices, as Gregory of Sinai orders us to do: "Lift up your eyes to heaven and stretch out your hands toward God for these two vices, fornication and acedia, are the most terrible." To prayer add spiritual reading and manual labor as much as is possible, for the one and the other are of great benefit in fighting against such vices.

Still it happens that even through these exercises there is no relief from such a vice as vicious as that of acedia. Then one must exert great need for strength and with all force cry out in prayer. But against the spirit of ingratitude and despair pray in this manner: "Begone, Satan. I will adore my Lord God and him alone will I serve; and every bitter and sorrowful cross I accept with a spirit of thanks and obedience from him for the cleansing of my sins as is written: 'The anger of God I accept, for I have sinned against him' (Mt 4:10; Mi 7:9). Satan, may your ingratitude and despair return to you and rest on your own head. The Lord will say to you: 'Depart from me! God has made me in his own image and likeness. Let him overthrow and destroy you!'"

If after this the evil spirit does not cease its attacks, direct your thoughts to another subject, divine or human. Above all, let the soul, wishing to please God, stand steadfast and exercise patience and trust in God, as St. Macarius writes. For the cunning of the evil enemy attacks us by acedia in order to deprive the soul of any trust in God. But God never allows any soul who relies on him to fall and be vanquished, for he knows all our weaknesses. If a person knows what burden to place on his ass, mule, or camel, and he places upon each animal according to its strength; if a potter knows just how long to hold his vessels in the fire in order to form them, not too long, not too short a time, so that they do not crack, but they come forth well shaped and not misshapened; if such people are sufficiently knowledgeable in their works, is it not all the more wise to believe God sees what temptation a soul is able to withstand in order to bring it through temptations to the heavenly Kingdom, not only to merit future glory, but also even now to enjoy the consolation of the Holy Spirit? Knowing this we must bear all with patience and tranquillity as we sit in our cells.

3. The Need to Converse with Saintly Persons

It is true that at times we will feel a great need to converse with and receive instruction from someone skilled and edifying in the spiritual life, as St. Basil the Great says: "Often when acedia attacks the soul, it can be dispelled by leaving one's cell and engaging in wholesome and pure measured conversation. A monk can be strengthened and refreshed to return with more zeal to devote oneself to the pious, ascetical practices." But the Fathers teach that if we can bear this struggle in silence without leaving the cell, this is better, as they attest out of their own experiences.

g. VAINGLORY

We must be very vigilant against the spirit of vanity because it hinders all of our intentions with all kinds of allurements. It impedes the monk's true progress by corrupting all his actions so that, no longer ordered to God, they become motivated by vainglory and the desire to seek to please others. For this reason we must constantly examine our thoughts and feelings to see: Are our actions done for God and for our spiritual benefit? It is necessary to avoid any kind of praise from people and to recall to mind the words of holy David: "The Lord has scattered the bones of them who please men" (Ps 52:6) in order to drive away any kind of self-flattering temptation that may inspire one to act in order to please others.

Let us be grounded firmly in our thoughts, so that we do all things in accord with God's will. If anyone so conducts himself with his deepest desire, he will be victorious when the temptation of vainglory should rise up against his will out of weakness. But let him confess by praying to the Lord. Let him transform such a thought by humbling and debasing himself. And he who sees all of our hearts will forgive us when our soul is totally open before him and we bring every movement of our soul to him. He will not blame us for having such thoughts.

1. How to Battle Vainglory

When we battle the temptation to vainglory we must act in this way: When we feel the stirring to seek self-praise for whatever reason, let us then remember our tears and recall the terrifying Last Judgment as we stand before God, by praying some of our special prayers, if we have any that are effective. If not, let us picture our final departure from this world and thus drive away such shameless vanity. Still, if we cannot get rid of the temptation in this way, let us fear at least the humiliation which will follow such vainglory. For, as St. John Climacus teaches, "He who exalts himself while still on this earth will not escape being humbled even before the life to come."

If ever someone should begin to praise us, or if it comes from the activity of our invisible enemy tempting our blinded heart and he begins to implant such a thought in us that we are worthy of such honor and preference since we deserve to occupy such lofty places, at once let us recall to ourselves the number and gravity of our sins or only one of them, the most foul. Let us picture it vividly in our mind and say then to ourselves: "Judge whether such actions are worthy of praise and honor." Then we should see at once the impossibility of any praise at all and the internal enemy is driven away.

And if you have no kind of grave and shameful sins to recall, ponder how wide, perfect, and far-sweeping is each commandment of God and you will see that your ascetical life is like a mere drop of water compared to the immensity of the sea. And so we constantly must be on our guard to keep ourselves free of vainglory. If, however, we will not be careful, but often we should yield to such vain temptations, they will take root in us and give birth to disdain and pride, the beginning and end of all evil.

h. PRIDE

What is there to say about haughtiness and pride? There are various names for these, but in substance all are really only one. This applies equally to pride and haughtiness, arrogance and boasting of oneself. All of these refer to the same vice, as the holy Writings teach: "God resists the proud" and "He holds in abomination every puffed-up soul" (Prv 3:34, 16:5), and such is called "uncleaned." God is his enemy and his soul is dead and unclean before God. From where, how, when can such a person find any assistance? From whom can he obtain mercy? Who can purify him? How painful it is even to speak of this. Anyone who surrenders himself to this vice becomes to himself a devil and his own enemy. He carries in himself the seeds of his own destruction.

1. Fear and Trembling Before the Lord

For this reason we should be filled with fear and trembling at the thought of this vice of pride. We must drive it out of ourselves completely, always mindful that without God's help, we could never do the slightest good act. Remember, if God forsakes us, we become like a leaf shaking in the wind or like dust tossed about in a storm. The devil hurls at us insults and we become mere puppets in his hands. We are made into a weeping sight before other persons. Realizing this, let us take all the measures to live our life in humility.

For the person wishing to learn how to acquire humility (for this is a divine science), he must first consider himself to be lower than all others, that is, he must regard himself as the worst and most perverse of all creatures, because he has lost the harmony innate in every natural creature and he is now worse than all the devils, who pursue and conquer us.[39] Secondly, he must always choose the last place, both at table and community gatherings with the brethren. He should also wear the poorest clothes. He must show a preference for the most menial types of work. In meeting a brother he must bow lowly and reverently to each one. He should love silence. Let him not seek to be brilliant in conversations. He should flee from any spirit of arguing with and contradicting others. Let him not show himself off in his works nor to do anything ostentatiously.

He ought not to insist on his own opinion even though it may seem to be quite correct. For as the Fathers taught: "For novices the inner person is formed according to external actions." St. Basil the Great teaches: "If the external person is not well disciplined, so also never believe that the inner person will be disciplined."[40]

2. Humility in Words

St. Gregory of Sinai says that "vanity and pride are to be overturned, but humility is born and grows from the roots. This growth is expressed for example in one's words. Do I truly know the sins of others, what kinds they are and truly how often have they so sinned? Are there in the world sinners whose sins are equal to mine, let alone exceeding mine? No, my soul, you and I are worse than all men, we are dust and ashes under their feet. How can I help considering myself the most despicable of all creatures, when they behave according to the order of their nature, whereas I, owing to my innumerable sins, have sunk below my nature? Truly animals and beasts are purer than I, sinner that I am, for I am the lowest of all since I have brought myself down into hell and am lying there even before death. Who does not know or feel that a sinner is worse even than the demons, since he is their subject and their slave, even here sharing their prison in the outer darkness? A man possessed by demons is truly worse than the demons. You dwell in the abyss of hell even before death. How dare you delude yourself and call yourself righteous when through evil deeds you have made of yourself a despicable sinner and a demon? Woe to your delusion and your error, you offspring of the devil, you unclean dog, condemned for this to fire and darkness."[41]

3. Temptations to Pride Common to Monks

The Fathers teach about the pride that is special to their state of life in the following types of proudful temptations. A monk may have worked hard and excelled in ascetical practices. He has put up patiently with much, holding back much anger on the way to virtue or for the sake of manifesting to others his pious life. But if one's pride is based on one's calling and preeminence of the monastery or the great number of brethren, the Fathers call this nothing but worldliness. But pride may rise among some monks who take pride in the monastery's acquiring of much land and monastic holdings, or of a monk's fame in the world and his acquaintances. What should I say of such as these?

There are such monks who have nothing to boast of before others than that they possess a fine voice well suited to chanting or eloquence in speech or reading aloud or reciting the Office. But what honor and praise should a monk merit from God for that which he has received, not from his own efforts, which does not depend on his own will, but what he has received as a gift from God? Still there are some monks who are vain in their artistic handicraft and they are just like those others already mentioned. Other monks take pride in being born from famous parents or having outstanding relatives well known in the world. Or they themselves before their entrance in the monastic life held places of honor and were numbered among the higher class of dignitaries. This is such absurd stupidity, for all such honors should remain hidden from others. For whoever has denounced the world should he turn around and be determined to seek any glory and to receive any honor from others, shame on him! Such monks should rather be ashamed and not be lifted up to be honored. For "seeking honor for a monk is never an honor, but shame. Their honor is a shame."[42]

4. How to Conquer Thoughts of Pride

If any monk because of his virtuous life should be attacked by temptations of vanity and pride, he must know that to conquer over such temptations, there is no more powerful weapon than to pray to the Lord God. Such a monk must struggle to cry out from the depths of his soul: "O, my Lord, Master, and God! Take from me this spirit of vanity and pride. Give to me, your servant, a spirit of humility!"

In place of such prideful thoughts he must reproach himself as we said above. For John Climacus teaches about the demons of vanity and pride: "There is only one thing in which we have no power to meddle and that is we cannot bear your blows. If you keep up a sincere condemnation of yourself before the Lord, you can count us weak as a cobweb."[43] Furthermore, St. Isaac tells us about pride that it is not really pride when a proud thought enters our mind without our holding it in its power, for God will not judge nor punish one for unwillful temptations.[44] If a monk, as soon as a proud thought should appear to the soul, immediately drives away from himself any passionate movement, there is no sin, but rather, this can be beneficial and for this God will not punish him. But authentic pride is when a monk receives such proudful temptations as something very good and worthy to be possessed and he does not consider them destructive and adverse to God's will. The height of pride is when this passion is acted out in words and actions. This cannot but be condemned. Thus do the Fathers also teach concerning vanity and in general all other individual vices.

6. On All Vices in General.

Against all evil thoughts we must call upon God for his help, for as St. Isaac taught, we are to fight against wicked thoughts. But there is no other help to accomplish this than by God's aid. Therefore, under the guidance of the instructions of Nil of Sinai, we must deliberately with sighs and tears pray to the Master Christ thus: "Have mercy on me, Lord, and do not allow me to perish. Have mercy on me for I am weak! Put to shame, Lord, the demon that is attacking me. O my Trust, protect me with your shade, O Lord, during the day in my struggle against the devil. Battle with me as I battle against the enemy, O Lord, and arm me with thoughts of meekness by your silence, O Word of God!"

Or according to the instruction of blessed Theodore the Studite, we should pray against impure thoughts in the words of the prophet David: "Accuse my accusers, Yahweh. Attack my attackers," and so pray the entire Psalm 35. So also writes the hymn-writer [John Damascene]: "Gather together my distracted mind, Lord. Cleanse my heart, most frozen and vice-prone, of such an unsightly creature as I am. Give me repentance, as you did to Peter; as to the publican, grant me a spirit of contrite sighing. Like the adulterous woman, grant me tears that I may cry unto you." Help me and deliver me from such base thoughts! For like the waves of the sea, so my wickednesses rise up to drown me and, like a boat about to be shipwrecked, so I am being overburdened by my thoughts. But, O Lord, bring me to a peaceful harbor through repentance and save me! I am seriously afflicted because of the weakness of my mind, not wishing a true change in my life. For this reason I cry out to you: "O holy Trinity without beginning, help me and place within me good thoughts and feelings!"

Thus choosing from the holy Writings what is helpful against each vice and needed in each moment, in like manner we will call on God for help against all temptations and he will respond and drive them away. Since we are weak and cannot by our own strength resist such evil thoughts, we must call upon God for his aid according to the examples of the holy Fathers by calling on his name according to the teachings of the holy Writers. We should say to each temptation: "May God forbid you any entrance" (Jude 9) and also: "Let all my enemies, discredited, in utter torment, fall back in sudden confusion" (Ps 6:10).

Thus I may be instructed in the laws of my God. Let us learn from the example of that starets [elder, spiritual guide] who taught: "Depart from me, evil one, and come, Beloved!" One of the brethren overheard him speaking and thought that he was speaking with someone and so he asked him with whom he was conversing. The Elder answered: "I was driving out evil thoughts and calling the good ones to come to me." We too should speak in a similar way whenever it will be necessary and proper for us.

7. On the Remembrance of Death and the Last Judgment. How to Learn to Cultivate Such Thoughts in Our Hearts.

The Fathers say that in our mental activity it is most helpful to have ever before us the remembrance of death and the Last Judgment. Philotheus of Sinai insists on this activity and even suggests a rule and an order of doing it. He teaches: "From morning until dinner focus your remembrance upon God, that is, by praying and guarding the heart. And then giving thanks to God, focus your mind by meditating upon death and judgment." Whoever dedicates himself to this meditation surely will experience the fulfillment of the Lord's words: "This very night the angels will demand your soul" (Lk 12:20). "For every unfounded word you will answer on judgment day" (Mt 15:19). Or the words of the Apostles: "The end is approaching" (1 Pt 4:7). "The day of the Lord will come as a thief in the night" (1 Thes 5:2). "For all the truth about us will be brought out in the law court of Christ" (2 Cor 5:10). "The word of God judges, not only our deeds and words, but also the thoughts of our hearts" (Heb 4:12).

Remembrance of One's Last Day

The first of the Fathers of the desert, St. Antony the Great, says: "We must keep ever in our mind what we should be concentrating on if we in this given day were not to live to its end." St. John Climacus writes, "Remember your last day and you would never sin." And again he enjoins us to remember always our death. St. Isaac the Syrian said: "Always carry in your heart, man, the remembrance of your departure from this life." And all the saints personally always did the same and enjoined on others, who also were eager for salvation, to be attentive to this. And not only the saints, but also the wise, secular philosophers agree that the remembrance of one's death is very important for moral perfection. But how can we, who are bound to our passions and so weak, learn to keep this thought ever present?

St. Isaac taught: "For perfection and integration the remembrance of our death and judgment is a gift and a supernatural grace from God." Our inconsistency, our distractions, cause a great impediment. We plainly forget to recall death, judgment, hell, and eternal happiness. We often think of these; sometimes we converse with others about death. But deep within our heart we cannot seem to deepen this thought and remain rooted in its reality. But even with our good will and unceasing efforts, only with God's help and our work and in time can we make progress in this matter.[45]

But for one who really wishes to make progress, he must act in this way: Let him vividly recall what was taught above. Let him consider the greatest necessity and help it is to remember his own death. Let him be convinced that, just as bread is the most needed of all foods to survive, so also remembrance of one's death is the most required of all virtues. How is it possible that a hungry person will not recall the thought of bread? So also for one desirous of salvation, it should be possible to have always in mind the remembrance of his death. Thus have the Fathers taught.

Furthermore, let your mind focus itself and concentrate on various terrifying types of death, as the saints suggested in their writings, as, for example, Gregory the Preacher and many others. It is beneficial and helpful for us to recall to mind some of the different types of deaths which we have witnessed or have heard of as having recently happened. How many such types of deaths happened quite unexpectedly—not only to laypersons, but also we know certain monks who were thriving and enjoying a healthy life with the hope of living a long life, only to have been suddenly overcome by death. Many of these were overtaken so very quickly by death that they did not even have time to say the final dying prayers for forgiveness.

Suddenness of Death

Some of these were struck by death where they were standing or sitting. Others died at table while they were eating and drinking. Suddenly they breathed their last breath. Others ended their lives while walking along a road. Still others fell asleep into the eternal sleep in bed where they lay, seeking a bit of rest for their bodies. Some, as we know, in their last hour experienced frightening and tormenting visions that were terrifying to them.

Bringing all this to our memory, let us reflect: Where now are our friends and acquaintances we knew while they were alive? What has been left now of the honors and fame they enjoyed while they were alive? Where is the power they possessed? Of what profit now are their riches and abundant possessions of all kinds? Have they not all been changed into ashes, smoke and dust? Let us recall the teaching of the composer of liturgical verses [St. John Damascene] on this subject: "What earthly pleasure can remain untouched by sadness? Or what glory attained on earth will remain incorruptible? Every stack of hay is of the weakest stuff and all dreams are most illusory. In one hour death receives all these. Truly all is vanity in this life! What can we take with us after death? No one can take into the next life the riches of this life. The fame of this world will be snatched from us for with the coming of death all these things will be destroyed."

And so, reflect on the vanities of this world to which during our life we are so attached and for which we work in vain. The road on which we journey is so short. Our life is nothing but smoke, vapor, a cloud, and ash. It appears and quickly vanishes. Even to call it a road does not have much meaning. In the words of St. John Chrysostom, it is less than a cobweb. He reflects: "Take, for example, a traveler who wishes to make a journey to a certain country. He goes there. But if he decides not to go, he does not go. And when he arrives at an inn, he knows when he arrives and when he intends to leave. Let's say he arrives at the inn in the evening. He then leaves in the morning. But if he changes his mind, he may take his time or hasten on his journey. But we, whether we wish it or not, must depart from this world. And we do not know the time of our departure. And it is not up to our free will to wish to stay on this earth for some added time, even though we indeed would like that. But death's dreadful mystery comes suddenly to us indeed. The soul is violently separated from the body. The thread of their natural union is sundered by the will of God."

And what will we then do if earlier we did not think of that hour, if we did not prepare in advance for it, but we would find ourselves even unprepared? In that bitter hour, we reflect: What a struggle for the soul to leave the body! What weeping! But nothing will help us. No one can have mercy on us. The soul will raise its eyes to the angels and beg for help in vain. The body will stretch out its hands to people but no help will come from anyone, but from God and one's good works.

Vanity of Vanities

And so, meditate on the brevity of our earthly life. Let us be concerned with the hour of our death by not giving ourselves over to the worries of this world and to unprofitable cares. "Every person crumbles to dust," says Holy Scripture (see Jb 34:15). In spite of the fact that we and the whole world seemingly are in charge of ourselves, nevertheless, let us abide in the grave, taking nothing there of this world, neither beauty nor glory nor power; no honors nor any other temporal good creature. Let us look into the grave and what do we see? We see our created beauty, now without form, without glory, nothing good remaining. Seeing our bones, do we know to whom they belonged? Was he a king, a beggar, honorable or without honor? All that the world considers beautiful, powerful, turns again into nothingness as a beautiful flower fades and dies, as a shadow passes by. Thus all mankind must also pass away. Feel this instability and call out to your soul: "Oh, how strange, why does this remain ever for us a mystery? How were we brought into bodily existence? Why do we return to dust in death? Truly, this is the will of God, for so it was written, after Adam's fall, he fell under sickness, subject to every woe. Death entered creation and it overcame us too. But the foreseen death of the Lord and his ineffable wisdom teach us that, by his coming, he overcame the serpent and gave us resurrection, transferring his slaves and servants into life everlasting."[46]

Thus we should keep in mind the thought of our Lord's Second Coming and our resurrection and the Last Judgment, recalling all that our Lord taught about these future events found in his Gospel as the divinely inspired Matthew wrote: "For then there will be great distress such as, until now, since the world began, there never has been, nor ever will be again. And if that time had not been shortened, no one would have survived; but shortened that time shall be, for the sake of those who are chosen. If anyone says to you then, 'Look, he is in the desert,' do not go there; 'Look, he is in some hiding place,' do not believe it; because the coming of the Son of Man will be like lightning striking in the east and flashing far into the west. Wherever the corpse is, there will the vultures gather. Immediately after the distress of those days the sun will be darkened, the moon will lose its brightness, the stars will fall from the sky, and the powers of Heaven will be shaken. And then the sign of the Son of Man will appear in Heaven; then too all the peoples of the earth will beat their breasts; and they will see the Son of Man coming on the clouds of Heaven with power and great glory. And he will send his angels with a loud trumpet to gather his chosen from the four winds, from one end of heaven to the other" (Mt 24:21–31).

But the beloved disciple of the Lord, the inspired John, hands down the Lord's following words: "The hour will come, in fact, it is already here, when the dead will hear the voice of the Son of God, and all who hear it will live," and "Those who have done good will rise to life; and those who have done evil, to condemnation" (Jn 5:25, 29).

The Last Judgment

And again the evangelist Matthew writes: "When the Son of Man comes in his glory, escorted by all the angels, then he will take his seat on his throne of glory. All the nations will be assembled before him and he will separate men one from another as the shepherd separates sheep from goats. He will place the sheep on his right hand and the goats on his left. Then the King will say to those on his right hand, 'Come, you whom my Father has blessed, take for your heritage the kingdom prepared for you since the foundation of the world. For I was hungry and you gave me food; I was thirsty and you gave me to drink; I was a stranger and you welcomed me; naked and you clothed me; sick and you visited me; in prison and you came to see me.' Then the virtuous will say to him in reply, 'Lord, when did we see you hungry and feed you; or thirsty and give you drink? When did we see you a stranger and make you welcome; naked and clothe you; sick or in prison and go to see you?' And the King will answer, 'I tell you solemnly, insofar as you did this to one of the least of these brothers of mine, you did it to me.' Next he will say to those on his left hand, 'Go away from me, with your curse upon you, to the eternal fire prepared for the devil and his angels. For I was hungry and you never gave me food; I was thirsty and you never gave me anything to drink; I was a stranger and you never made me welcome, naked and you never clothed me, sick and in prison and you never visited me.' Then it will be their turn to ask, 'Lord, when did we see you hungry or thirsty, a stranger or naked, sick or in prison, and did not come to your help?' Then he will answer, 'I tell you solemnly, insofar as you neglected to do this to one of the least of these, you neglected to do it to me.' And they will go away to eternal punishment, and the virtuous to eternal life" (Mt 25:31–46).

What, my brethren, can be more fearful and terrifying than to hear the answer of that judgment when we shall see all the sinners and those who have never repented, by God's just judgment, being sent into eternal tortures as they, with unspeakably cruel trembling, scream out and bitterly weep? How shall we not be touched and not weep when we picture in our imagination the terrifying and cruel torments which Holy Scripture describes as everlasting fire, the outer reaches of darkness, the deep abyss, the dragon, cruel and vigilant, the gnashing of teeth, and the other sufferings awaiting those who have sinned and by their works have incurred the wrath of the all-good God?

Giving an Account of One's Life

And from among these sinners am I not the first of the wretches? What will we, guilty of so many sins, do then when we hear God call the blessed of his Father into the heavenly Kingdom and he separates from them sinners, casting them into torments? What answer will we give? What will we say when all our acts are brought forward, all our secret words, thoughts, everything ever done secretly in day or night, now revealed to everyone? What shame will come over us? To deny the shameful deeds will be impossible. Speaking of that fear and awfulness of the Second Coming of the Lord and his terrifying judgment, some Fathers say that if it would then be possible to die the whole world would die from fear.

What fear, brethren, will overtake us when we stand before the throne and they open the books, when God will sit on the tribunal of judgment in glory and the angels will stand about him in trembling awe? Truth will convict and the greatest fear and shame will pierce through the souls of the sinners. It will not be so for the righteous. They in joy and happiness will enter into the heavenly palace and receive the reward for their good works.

It is for this reason that we should entertain a holy fear and terror and deepen always in our mind this thought of the judgment. If our heart would not desire to do so, we must force it to ponder this subject and cry out: "Woe are you, O wretched soul, for the time of your departure from this body is close at hand. How much longer will you not cease from your evil works? How long will you continue to live in such dissolution? Why will you not be touched by terror at the terrible judgment of the Savior? What answer will you give or what will you say then in your own defense? See, your deeds are ever before you, covering you and witnessing against you!"

Have Mercy on Me, O Master!

But, O soul, whatever time you still have, give up your shameless deeds and convert yourself to a noble life. Turn to the Lord and cry out with faith: "I have sinned, Lord. But I know your mercy and love for men. For this reason, I fall down and beg your goodness to grant me mercy, O Lord! For my soul will be confused and will be sick at my having turned away from my repentance and at my wicked bodily deeds. May the evil powers never capture me and cast me into darkness for my invisible and visible sins of my whole earthly life.

Have mercy on me, O Master, and do not let my soul ever look upon the ugly countenances of the evil demons, but let your radiant and most glorious angels receive me. You have authority to forgive sins. Forgive me my sins. Let my sin never again be before you for because of my weakness I have sinned in word and in deed and in thought, deliberately and indeliberately. May I turn toward you when I am divested of my body and not be found with any filth on the image of my soul. And may the hand of the dark prince of this world never receive me, a sinner, and drag me into the depths of hell, but may you stand before me and be my Savior and Protector!

Have mercy, O Lord, on my soul, so stained by the passions of this life, and receive it, purified by repentance and confession. And by your power conduct me before your divine judgment seat. And when you come down, God, upon this earth in glory, you will sit on your throne, O Merciful One, to pass your just judgment; we shall all stand naked before you, like the condemned. May we stand before your wise judgment. When you will begin to examine our sinfulness, then, O most Good One, do not expose my secret thoughts, nor disgrace me before the angels and all other human beings, but spare me, O God, and show me your mercy.

As much as I meditate on your judgment, O Good One, I am filled with fear for the day of the terrifying judgment. My conscience condemns me and the evil of my deeds fills me with overwhelming remorse. I am gripped with confusion as to how I shall answer you, O Immortal King, for I incurred your wrath. How shall I look upon you in the terrible Last Judgment with such boldness, for I have been filthy and a fornicator? But, O Lord, good and compassionate Father, only-begotten Son and Holy Spirit, have mercy on me and free me then from the inextinguishable fire and allow me to stand at your right hand, O just Judge.[47]

8. On Tears and About Those Wishing to Acquire This Gift of Tears.

So by praying and meditating in a similar way as described above, if God should give us the grace of tears, we must not restrain ourselves, but weep as much as possible according to our strength and power, for the Fathers have taught that such weeping delivers us from the eternal fire and other impending torments. But if we are not able to weep much, we ought to seek, even if they are only a few tears, to shed them with earnest efforts, according to the words of St. John Climacus.[48] He assures us that our good Judge regards our tears exactly as he does all our works, and judges them, not by their quantity, but by their quality and in proportion to our strength and ability. "I have seen," he writes, "some persons shedding only very few drops of tears, but they poured forth as though they were blood with a sickening feeling. I also saw others whose abundant tears flowed out as from a fountain, freely, but without a sense of inner sickness. I have seen the first and second types and I judge them, not by the quantity of tears of the person weeping, but by the painful feeling in his heart. I think God judges likewise."

Praying for the Gift of Tears

But if by reason of our weakness or our carelessness or for whatever other reason we are unable and can weep only a bit, we should not give up or become discouraged, but let us be grief-stricken and sigh and lament and be filled with sadness at our inability to weep. Let us keep trying with a healthy hope for, as St. Isaac says: "Suffering and anguish of the spirit exceed any amount of bodily deeds." St. John Climacus also is in agreement with him when he discerns: "Some monks, wishing, but not receiving the gift of tears, interiorly lament and weep. This is equivalent to the external gift of tears, even though the tears do not appear visibly."

It even happens in some cases, as St. Isaac teaches, that the absence of physical tears may be due to some sort of weakness and even a certain bodily weakness. And Symeon the New Theologian discourses in his conferences on tears, as he teaches us to weep always, but only by the movement of the special and ineffable gaze of God. Otherwise, by forcing one's weakness of nature, the source of tears will diminish. This is found also in Holy Scripture where David the psalmist notes that exterior tears should flow from interior weeping: "My sacrifice to you, God, is this broken spirit. You will not scorn this crushed and broken heart" (Ps 51:19). And thus we must groan in our thoughts, by being full of sorrow, and seek tears with a broken and humbled heart.

How to Seek the Gift of Tears

To seek tears we must do as the holy Writings enjoin upon us if we truly wish to have this gift.[49] From among these Fathers Symeon the New Theologian teaches that if our soul is in such a disposition, namely, really understands its true nature and its actual fallen nature and is hence filled with deep sorrow and compunction at its estrangement from God, it cannot but weep bitterly with tears. Furthermore, Symeon the New Theologian writes with great exactness in these matters as he recalls the words of the psalmist David and the writings of John Climacus. One wishing this gift, or, better yet, desirous to learn this most important and superior lesson of the spiritual life, let him investigate further in the very book of Symeon the New Theologian and meditate well on what is laid out there and fulfill all, except never to war against one's natural, bodily constitution. For if you push the body powers too far, this is not helpful. For you will be forcing the weak body beyond its strength and weakness will follow. As St. Isaac teaches: "You heap confusion upon confusion on the soul and it becomes more troubled than before." In this he agrees with the other Fathers.

But we must understand what the Fathers intend here by "real weakness." It is not the adverse and self-destructive weakness. All of us must always use necessary force against this, as St. Symeon teaches. If we have not attained a high degree of perfection in this matter, then let us strive to attain at least a small degree of tears. And let us beg this of the Lord God with an aching heart. For the

Fathers have taught that tears are a gift, one of the greatest gifts, and they enjoin us to ask it of the Lord.[50] Thus blessed Nil of Sinai teaches: "Before all other gifts of God pray for the gift of tears." And blessed Gregory, the most holy Pope of Rome, writes: "Whoever lives habitually in doing good works and has been found worthy to receive some gifts from God, but has not yet received the gift of tears, ought to pray for the ability to weep, either through the fear of the terrifying Last Judgment or through his longing for the heavenly Kingdom. The first comes by repenting over one's evil past deeds and the second by kneeling before the cross of Christ, seeing him suffering for us, our crucified Savior."[51] Pope Gregory presents a parable from Holy Scripture: "Sitting on an ass, she [Axa, the daughter of Caleb] asks her father for a piece of land with irrigation. 'You gave me dry land,' she tells him. 'Give me some with water as in the valley.' And the father gave her water in the mountains and water in the valley." By Axa, explains the holy Father Gregory, is meant the human soul, sitting on the ass, that is, the bodily movements. He explains that Axa, sighing and asking for land with water from her father, is how we must, with great grief of heart and with sighing, ask our life-giving Father for the gift of tears.[52] And other saints agree with him.

How to Pray for this Gift

How are we to ask and pray for this gift of tears and how are we even to begin? Is there any other way than that found in Holy Scripture? It is not enough merely for us to reflect upon ourselves, but it is enough to reflect upon the prayers found in the inspired Holy Scriptures as well as those prayers found in the writings of the saints.[53]

Some Prayers of the Holy Fathers

Take, for example, the prayer composed by Andrew of Crete: "Where shall I begin to lament my wretched life's actions? What

100

shall I set for first-fruit of this my lamentation? O Merciful One, grant me, O Lord, tears of remorse that I may weep before you, the Creator of all and our Maker and our God. Before you, O Savior, I lie completely revealed; how much I have sinned with my sorry soul and my brutish flesh; grant that with your help, I may be strengthened to throw off my past sinfulness and bring to you tears of repentance."[54]

Germanus of Constantinople: "O my God, Creator of the whole world, my Maker, the one who brought forth the water that gushed out from the struck rock, and the one who sweetened the bitter waters at Meribah, give to the pupils of my eyes fountains of tears, cover my head with your cleansing waters and accompany my journeys with clouds always pouring forth abundant tears! For the impurity of my thoughts and my soiled soul demand, O Master, the sprinklings and cleansings that come from your love for mankind. The eyes of my heart thirst for the unceasing rain of the waters of tears, like a lake or spring that purifies the soul." St. Ephrem the Syrian: "Give, O Master, to me, unworthy though I am, the gift of continued tears in order to enlighten my heart so that I may pour out fountains of tears with sweetness in pure prayer as the long listing of my sins so demands such poor tears so that the fires of retribution for my sins may be extinguished by this simple weeping."[55] Symeon the New Theologian: "O Lord and Giver of life to all creatures, grant me hands lifted up for your help and cleanse the stains of my soul and give me tears of penance, loving tears out of love, tears of salvation, tears that clean the darkness of my mind, making me light so that I may see you, Light of the world, Enlightenment to my repentant eyes."[56] St. John Damascene, hymn-writer: "O Christ, King of all creatures, give me hot tears so that I may weep for my soul and for all its destructive evils. Give me, O Christ, a cloud of tears of divine humility that I may abundantly weep and be cleansed of my stains, especially for the pleasures I have sought, so that I may appear before you completely cleansed. Give me tears, O God, as once of old you gave them to the repentant harlot."

And many other comparable verses and hymns similar to these sentiments that are found in the holy Writings should come forth with sincerity out of the depths of our soul, begging for tears and

101

often praying to the Lord that he grant us the grace of such tears, which, according to the words of St. Isaac the Syrian, is the best and most excellent of all other gifts. If we ardently seek this, by it we will come into purity of the soul and become capable of receiving all other spiritually good gifts.

Other Ways of Weeping without Tears

There are certain persons who have not yet obtained completely the gift of tears, but they do find it in various ways. Some do it through contemplating the secret beauties of the Architect and Lover of mankind, God; others through reading the lives of the saints and their teachings; others by the Jesus Prayer; others come to this compunction from certain prayers composed by saints; others pray some canons and *tropars*;[57] others through remembrance of their sins; others from the remembrance of death and judgment; others through longing for the future joys of Heaven; and so by various ways they obtain the gift of tears. If anyone by any such subject is aroused to tears, he must meditate on how to retain this weeping until the tears no longer come. For one wishing to be delivered from sins is delivered from them by weeping, and one wishing to keep the self from sin is kept so by weeping, said the Fathers.[58]

The way of repentance with its fruit consists in this, so that in times of attack by evil spirits, and even before every suggestion from the enemy by way of thoughts, let weeping by God's grace be our strength. And if we will pray with wisdom, the Lord will not tarry in giving us rest and peace. St. Symeon the New Theologian teaches: "All virtues are similar to an army, but meekness and weeping are exalted as a king and a general. For weeping from one side arms us and teaches us and strengthens us to fight against the enemy in all of our undertakings. On the other hand, it protects us against any destructive antagonist. But if it so happens that our mind is heavily burdened with any sort of simple thoughts which may excite us through our senses by hearing and seeing certain pleasant things, or through any sad occasions that affect our emotions, we should convert even such feelings that arouse us to natural tears into tears that are spiritual and salvific. We can turn our mind to praising God and acknowledging his perfections and works, or by meditating upon death, judgment, future torments in the life to come, and so forth, and in this way, let us weep tears of grace." St. John Climacus teaches that to convert natural tears to spiritual tears is worthy of praise. However, he calls our attention to the fact that if our soul, by the grace of God, is humbled and weeps tears spontaneously without our willing them, this is nothing other than a visitation of God. These are genuine tears of grace-given piety. Such tears must be cherished as the apple of our eye and we should yield ourselves to them as long as they persist, because they have a greater power and really can help better to uproot and destroy sins and vices than those tears that we bring about by our own effort and by various means or cleverness on our part.

When we are attentive to ourselves, that is, by keeping guard over our heart, there begins to operate within us by God's grace the spiritual power of prayer, manifested by warming the heart within us and filling the soul with joyful radiance throughout our entire being. It comforts us by inflaming us with an indescribable love of God and other human beings. It enlightens our mind and pours out into our innermost being the feeling of joy.

Value of the Gift of Tears

Then tears flow abundantly and automatically without any effort on our part, springing forth, as St. John Climacus teaches, like the tears of an infant that weeps and at the same time laughs, that is, it rejoices spiritually expressing this joy also on its face. May the Lord grant us such tears! For us beginners, weak and inexperienced, there is no other consolation than this. And when this is given, by God's grace, this gift of grace—that is, tears—begins to increase in us. Then the battle with the enemy becomes easier and temptations are quelled and calmed and the mind is fed with an abundantly nourishing food and it delights in prayer. From the depths of the heart pours out a certain ineffable sweetness, reacting on the whole body, and every sick and diseased sense reacts on all the body members with an exulting joy.[59] "See what consolation flows out of weeping," says St. Isaac, "according to the Lord's words, 'given to each according to the grace that is in him' (Rom 12:3, 6). Then a person feels a joy not found anywhere else in this world. This is completely unknown to anyone except to those who dedicate themselves completely with their whole soul to this spiritual work."[60]

9. On How to Cultivate the Gift of Tears.

When the Lord by his grace deigns to grant to us the gift of tears and to cry aloud, or when he empowers us to be skilled in "pure prayer," then let us generously guard ourselves against any spirit of anger and any other evil attacks. For our enemy in such special time either tries to disturb us with interior thoughts and lustful movements or cunningly from outside wages a war and a riot against us in order that our work be interrupted and we commit depravities.

St. John Climacus teaches: "As soon as you begin to pray purely and with great attention, quickly you will find yourself overcome by the enemy and on fire with some anger. What cunning of our enemies! For this reason every good work, but especially prayer, must always be done with as much attention as possible along with deep affection and after prayer you will conquer such passion, anger, and other emotions so harmful to the soul. For beginners the absence of anger is maintained and guarded against by tears, as if one had built a protective dike against the enemy. And if we open up the dike or do not use it properly at once all hell breaks loose! As Nil of Sinai, the Faster, says: "The devil becomes extremely jealous seeing a person praying, and by every sort of snares forces his mind away from prayer by constantly stirring up in his memory various phantasms and bringing about in the body all sorts of passions in order to put a stop to any earnest asceticism and prayerful relationship to God."

But when this most evil spirit, after many clever deceits employed by the devil, cannot prevent such powerful prayer of the one praying so extraordinarily, at that time the devil diminishes his actions and turns to a greater evil used to attack the monk in prayer. This he does by tormenting him with anger against a certain person, or by any stratagem, to deprive the soul of such a gift of prayer. Or he attacks the monk's emotions with a certain false sweetness to torture his mind. Therefore, pray as is befitting. Wait for what is not proper and stand manfully with courage as you guard your fruit, for you must first hold firmly in what you are doing and protect yourself in doing it. So, by working and toiling do not cease in your guarding of what you have acquired by toil and work. For without this attentiveness you will never benefit from prayer.

It is clear that when touching on "toil and attentiveness" the holy Father [St. Nil of Sinai] appeals to the words of the history of Adam in paradise, for Scripture says: "God made Adam and placed him in a paradise to cultivate and take care of it" (Gn 2:15). He means by the work of paradise, prayer. But guarding one's heart comes after prayer. "Taking care" refers to guarding the fruit of prayer against any wicked and evil thoughts. And so, if the Lord deigns us worthy of his visitation by grace in the time of prayer, by granting us the gift of weeping and godly thoughts, let us guard ourselves from every kind of evil thoughts, especially vile words and deeds. Let us protect our emotions by being alert so that through these a battle will not be waged against us.

If because of a need against our own will, our soul might fall into some kind of phantasms, at once let us hasten to our Creator in prayer and he will drive them away. There is no more direct and hopeful way than this. And in this manner, with God's cooperation, we guard our soul in reverent fear of him. We will not let our mind be overcome and weakened from the attack of such thoughts or be overcome by any sort of vain pleasures; but, by distancing ourselves from all that might weaken our mind, we will not lose what we have gained by means of a meek and humble heart. By tears and prayer let us protect ourselves in such prudent wisdom.

10. On Renunciation and Genuine Detachment, Which Necessitates Dying to All Things.

This amazing practice, about which we have spoken, constantly demands a renunciation of all anxieties, which means a dying to attachments to all things created and an exercising of ourselves with total attention to the one, divine work, as the great Fathers have taught this wisdom from their own learned experiences.

St. Macarius the Great teaches: "Whoever wishes to come closer to the Lord and to be deigned worthy of eternal life and to become a temple of Christ and to be filled with the Holy Spirit in order to reach that stage of bringing forth the fruits of the Spirit and to be able to fulfill purely and without any blemish all the commandments of the Lord, he must begin before all else to believe powerfully in the Lord. He must zealously devote himself to observe his commands, by going against the spirit of the world in all things in order that his entire mind may be no longer occupied with anything of the visible world."

And it belongs primarily to him to concentrate on having only God ever before his eyes and to seek to be pleasing to him alone and unceasingly to be in prayer with faith in the expectation of the Lord as he vigilantly awaits his visitation and help. This should be the sole aim of his mind in each moment. Then, as he guards himself that no sin will live within him, he must apply himself in every good action to fulfill all the commands of the Lord. Above all, in never forgetting God's presence, remember as an image held before your mind the humility of the Lord and his life and meekness and his openness to the people. Let such a monk remain in prayer, always believing and begging that the Lord will come and dwell within him.

11. What Prudent Means to Take in Practicing This Exercise.

The monk must remember always the presence of God and the Lord will perfect and strengthen him in fulfilling all his commands. The Lord himself will dwell in his soul. And the monk will remember the Lord always and love him greatly. Then the Lord, seeing such determination on his part and his good resolve and seeing how he pushes himself constantly to remember the presence of the Lord and how his heart, even against his will, tends unceasingly toward the good, then the Lord will manifest to him his mercy and deliver him from his enemies and any sin living in him. He will fill him with his Holy Spirit.

And then without any effort and toil he will accomplish in all truth all the commands of the Lord. It would be better to say that the Lord himself keeps his own commands in him and he often brings forth then the fruits of the Spirit. And Basil the Great teaches: "The beginning of purity of the soul is silence." But the matter of silence according to the teachings of John Climacus is defined as the putting aside of all cares concerning affairs, not only unnecessary, but also good and praiseworthy things. Secondly, it is assiduous prayer and thirdly it is unremitting action of praying in the heart. Now when John Climacus refers to praiseworthy things, he does not refer to external affairs which are usually considered to be necessary in our time, such as overseeing farms and the administering of many properties and other involvements with the world. All this is for us stupid and not necessary.[61] But under the term of necessary affairs, John Climacus considers what concerns that which is edifying and helpful for the salvation of the soul—for example, conversations and encounters according to the proper time and in measure with Fathers and brothers who are spiritual and edifying. If such pious conversations revolve around their own affairs and take place without adequate prudence, then they tend toward what is not beneficial and necessary, but stupid, that is, they lead to pleasing indulgences, quarrels, arguments, prejudices, which may arise easily and unnoticeably from even pious conversations.

As St. John Climacus explains: "It is a natural thing that if you do not learn the letters of the alphabet, it is impossible for you to acquire the habit of reading books. The latter cannot be attained without the first preceding it. Simply put, if you have not learned to read, it is impossible to teach from books, to read, or to become a cantor. All the more, if you don't acquire the first condition, namely, to get rid of concerns about both noble and ignoble things, not to die to all that is of earth and the world, it is impossible for you to progress in chanting with wisdom. It is absurd to try to pray deeply interiorly. It is simply impossible to progress in works of the heart." And in another place he teaches: "A small hair in your eye can darken your vision, so also a small anxiety can destroy inner silence." And again: "For one who is tasting the fruit of prayer it is often only by one of his words his mind becomes dissipated, so that as he tries again to return to prayer no longer does he find what before he enjoyed in prayer."

St. Symeon the New Theologian teaches: "Let your life be one of silence and without any anxiety and toward all things be dead." And immediately after this instruction, he teaches on prayer and moderation. Blessed Isaac likewise teaches for those truly desirous of silence and purity of one's mind by prayer: "Distance yourself from the sight of the world and cut off any conversations. Refuse to receive in your cell any friends, even under the pretext of some good reasons, except those who are on your spiritual level of development and think as you do and share in your rich mystical gifts. Fear to trouble your soul by any conversation which often leaves traces for a long time, even after you have terminated such a conversation. We know this to be true from our own personal experiences."

Dangers from Conversations

It happens that after an intimate conversation with a friend, close and dear to us, even when it may have seemed to have been good, for some time after it still disturbs us and often is a great impediment to guarding the mind and hinders the mystical life.

In other places and even more forcefully, St. Isaac exhorts us: "Oh, what evil and what obstacles result from such meetings and conversations for those who sincerely live in solitude! O Brothers! Just as a great frost falling suddenly on a garden dries up all the fruit in the garden, so such human conversations, even if they do not last long or even if they seem to be geared to something good, the flowers of virtues dry up, which tenderly blossom forth only in silence.

This silence is where the flowers bloom and bring forth open, tender, young flowers that encircle the garden of the soul, which is planted and watered by the waters of repentance.

"Now if some vegetable plants can sprout forth, but bring something dead, so also such human conversations can put to death our mind, which is the root that allows the growth of virtues. And if such conversations are harmful with such persons among us, those who in their life are not completely dedicated and give only a small attention to their interior life, then how much more harmful for the soul are encounters and conversations with laypersons who are unconcerned and unreflective, to say nothing of the really worldly persons!

"Just as a man of culture and high morals when he becomes intoxicated forgets his good upbringing and disgraces his name, and calling in an ignoble way becomes a laughingstock before others because of his crude words and antics, a result of his drunkenness, so also purity of the soul is destroyed by such meetings and long conversations. Diligence in guarding the heart becomes weakened, sincerity in the pursuit of good works is diminished, and the soul's steady resolve is uprooted.

"And if such conversations take place not daily but from time to time, and if one does not control the door that guards the tongue and the sense of hearing, great harm comes to one seeking to live in silence since his mind becomes disturbed and weakened in spiritual pursuits. All the more, what can be said of those who continually are found together as constant companions, while not imposing any control on their tongue?"

"A person who turns to the world becomes deprived of life," says the same holy Father in another place. "I do not know what to say about a person who continually weeps with tears, with unconsoling wailing as he toils in his heart with compassion and brotherly love toward others." And again: "One contact with worldly persons can powerfully arouse and give food to the passions while weakening in the ascetic monk the love for asceticism and lessening his militant vigilance and love of wisdom." "For these reasons," says St. Isaac, "a monk must not dialogue on such topics since they wage a battle against him. But it is for him to run away from all kinds of such temptations and not allow himself any closeness to such since he exercises freedom in times of such temptations. For at the very time we turn toward God, we renew our covenant with him, promising to distance and cut ourselves off from all of this. And not only to cut oneself away from such a person, but not even to see any person of the world, neither hearing his words nor listening to any news about such a person." And still more like things does this holy man of God write, as do other saintly persons about this topic. Thus this truth is considered as most certain.

Proper Time and Measure for Doing One's Work

All such good and admirable works ought to be done in good time and in proper measure, as St. Basil the Great teaches. All our works should be done with good judgment, otherwise a work good in itself can be turned into something harmful, because it was not done at the right time and in the proper measure. But when right reason determines correctly the proper time and measure, then a very great benefit that is amazing results. And holy John Climacus, grounded on Sacred Scripture, teaches: "There is a time for everything under the heavens (Eccl 3:1), a time for our whole consecrated life for each of us. A time for silence and a time for quiet conversation. A time for unceasing prayer and a time for sincere recitation of the Office. And let us not be too eager to anticipate the proper time, otherwise we receive nothing when the proper time arrives. For there is a time to labor in cultivating good works and a time to reap a harvest of unspeakable graces."

Perfect Inner Silence Stamps Out Anxieties

When one of the brothers was reading to the great Barsanuphius from the *Paterikon*,[62] that one who truly desired to be saved had above all to suffer at the hands of the brethren living the common life, according to the example of the Lord, all sorts of vexations and insults and humiliations, and so forth, and thus reach perfect silence, which means "to hang on the cross"—that is, total mortification of himself to all that is of this earth and is worldly—the elder replied: "Truly the Fathers taught this for there can be no other way." To another, Barsanuphius taught: "First, if a person does not enter deeply into himself and does not have complete mastery over himself, silence begets only an exaggerated opinion of oneself. But if one does master himself, he will excel in humility."

And again he taught: "If you guard yourself in your behavior according to your means or character, know that you may lose even that which you possess. But hold yourself to moderation. Seek attentively the will of God. For whoever wishes with anxious zeal ahead of time to take on himself every external care and work, to such a one the common enemy prepares much greater troubles by robbing him of any peace. He leads him to such a condition in which he will be forced to admit: 'It were better for me not to have been born.'"

This saint taught thus because to such persons many illusions befall, as Gregory of Sinai teaches: "Many who are inexperienced in inner silence have in the past exposed themselves to allurements and even now such are still exposing themselves. Beginners and those who guide themselves, after many labors have reached the state of imageless, inner silence and now are the subject of derision and shame. For remember the presence of God, that is, mental prayer, is the highest of all our activities and is the mainstay of all virtues for the very reason that it is love of God. And anyone who without shame and with boldness seeks by their own power to come to God, seeking to converse with him frequently and to be intimate with him by his own power, he, I say, is quickly tricked into death if he opens himself up to the devil of death. For he strives to attain such a height in the spiritual life with pride and arrogance and anxiously before a proper time of development and he becomes unworthy of such a gift. Only the strong and perfect are in a position to fight alone in solitude against the demons by drawing the sword against them, 'which is the word of God' (Eph 6:17). The weak and the beginners who do not dare to fight alone in silence before they are ready take refuge in the fortress of fear and in the piety of the common life. In this way they escape death."

A Timely Progression in Sanctity

Hearing this teaching, we will be prudent and not arrogantly dare to attain too soon beyond our progress such a high level of asceticism so as not to incur harm and destroy our soul. By observing the proper time and the golden mean,[63] we will journey without danger and with proper hope. The holy Writings teach us that the middle path offers no obstacles.

And the best time for living the hermit's life of absolute silence comes only to the person who acquires wisdom by living the common life with other monks, for the middle way requires that a monk live with one other or two brothers, as St. John Climacus has written: "For one desirous to work for Christ there are three excellent ways to live the monastic life: either to live alone in solitude as a hermit, or to live in silence with one or two other monks or to live the common life in a coenobitic monastery." "Do not lean to the right or left, but walk by the way to the royal city," he added from Scripture (Dt 5:32; Nm 21:22).

From the aforementioned ways of living the monastic life the middle way, that is, the life of silence lived with one or two is, according to John Climacus's opinion, for most monks the most preferred. For, as he teaches, woe to the one who alone embraces the heremitical life. For when he is alone and falls into acedia or is overcome by sleep or by sloth or despair, there is no one at that time to lift him up and give him encouragement. In proof of this he offers the words of the Lord himself: "Where there are two or three gathered in my name, there am I among them" (Mt 18:20). Also, he presents the saying of the wise man: "Blessed are two over only one" (Eccl 4:9), that is, "Blessed be the Father with the Son through the cooperation of the Holy Spirit, when one leads the ascetical life together in them. Whoever seeks to wage the battle against the evil spirits without the help of another monk, such a one dies at their hands. He receives from the evil spirits the most dangerous of poisonous stings."

St. John Climacus taught that certain monks, noted for their good and moral lives, might find living with others not so beneficial. They are being directed by a teacher in silence as from a calm refuge they journey toward Heaven, not needing the usual instruction in how to combat temptations which come out of gossip and deceits found in living together with others. But for those who find this life of silence distasteful and are still being overcome by passions that attack the soul, the Fathers do not recommend that they embrace the life of silence, above all, of that of a hermit's life.

Advice to Those Still Battling the Passions

The passions that war against the soul are called vanity, self-opinion, malice, and others that stem from these. "A person who is dominated by these passions and nonetheless tries to live the life of silence is similar to a man who jumps out of a ship and thinks he can reach the shore safely on a mere plank," as Climacus said. But monks who are still battling against their carnal passions can embrace the solitary life, not simply as a more excellent way, but only at a proper time and if they are under the guidance of a spiritual guide. For solitude requires angelic power. For those still striving to overcome the passions of the soul, let them not dare to embrace the life of silence lest they lose what they have already acquired. We find many other holy and great Fathers who also taught this and acted in this way, as is seen from their Writings.

Thus does St. Isaac, more than all the Fathers, esteem silence and praises St. Arsenius the Great as the perfect hesychast. But even he had disciples and those who served him. So also Nil of Sinai and Daniel the Skete-Dweller and many others, as is attested to in their lives, and who also had disciples. And everywhere in the writings there are found praises and approval for the life of silence, but lived with one or two other monks. We have witnessed this style of life on the holy Mt. Athos and also in and around Constantinople, and in many other places, namely, a starets or elder living with one or two disciples or sometimes even three if there were a need. They would come for a certain time to him and engage in spiritual conversation. But for us, beginners and those who have not yet attained wisdom, let us be mutually enlightened and strengthened by each other as it is written: "A brother who helps another brother is like a fortified city" (Prv 18:19). And we have also an infallible teacher, the God-inspired Writings.

Therefore, it seems very fitting for us to live with one or two true brothers, united in one wisdom in doing the work of God. Let us learn to discover the will of God from the holy Writings. And if God should bestow more wisdom upon one, let him be an edification to the other brother. Fighting against the devils and the passions, let us help one another, as St. Ephrem teaches. And in this manner with God's grace, let us be directed in good works.

But when we wish to establish a hesychastic skete, above all, we must first build it upon prayer so that God may give us the property and all that is necessary for the skete's completion, as Climacus says, that is, a calm surroundings, a dwelling in one place, engaged in one work, in order that we determine at the beginning not to offer an occasion to our enemies to be ridiculed and an obstacle to others seeking the ascetical life. Let us be engaged in good works, firmly storing up the treasures of the grace of the Lord God and our Savior, Jesus Christ, by the prayers of our Queen, the Theotokos [Birth-Giver of God], and all the saints, who have excelled in living the virtuous, ascetical life.

We must realize that we should choose a place of silence so that we can separate ourselves from ourselves, from any unprofitable worry, idle gossip, and from any other factor unpleasing to God. Let us be engaged in keeping his commands. Let us provide all we need by our own labors. But if this is not sufficient, we may accept small alms, regarding them as a sign of God's goodness, but let us flee from any superfluity. Let us do that which is pleasing to God: chanting, prayer, reading and giving teachings on spiritual matters, manual work and labor in whatever work we are engaged in. And thus, little by little, according to each one's strength, we will glorify through our good works the Father and Son and Holy Spirit, one God in the Trinity, now and always and unto ages of ages. Amen.

I, so unwise, but having been helped by God's aid, according to the measure of my poor wisdom, have written this as a reminder to myself and others of one mind with me, who are in need of instruction, if they really desire it. It is not from myself, as I have said in the beginning, that I have written these things, but from the divinely inspired Writings of the holy Fathers, who were enlightened in wisdom.

For all that has been set down here is based on the witness found in the godly Writings. And if there should be anything in these writings not pleasing to God and not beneficial for the soul, due to my lack of wisdom, may it not be so. But may God's perfect and well-pleasing will be done. I only beg pardon on my part. If anyone should know any more wise and profitable ways of accomplishing these, may he do so and we will only rejoice.

And if anyone should find anything useful in these writings, may he pray for me, a sinner, so that I may receive mercy before God.

3. The Letters

LETTER I[1]

OF THE GREAT STARETS HERMIT

TO A BROTHER ASKING ABOUT TEMPTATIONS[2]

You have stirred up a praiseworthy desire, dearest friend, to hear the word of God, seeking to gain assurance for yourself. You are desirous to keep yourself from all evil and to learn how to do only good. But how much better it would have been for you to seek that from good and intelligent persons, instead of asking it of me, an irrational sinner. For I cannot claim to be among the ranks of learned men.[3] For this reason I declined and postponed for a long time, not because I was unwilling to be of assistance in fulfilling your good wishes, but rather on account of my lack of intelligence and my sinfulness. What indeed can I say, when I myself do not do anything good? What sort of understanding does a sinner have, besides that of his sin? But because you have so strongly insisted that I write you a letter on acquiring virtues (I know it is presumption on my part to do that which is beyond my capacity), I cannot ignore your request, otherwise you will be greatly offended. You asked about the temptations that have been occurring to you about your former worldly life. You yourself reflect from your own past experience: How many sorrows and how much seduction does this fleeting world contain? And what evil it rewards those who are enamored by it. How it laughs when those who served it must finally depart. Seemingly sweet, even caressing with pleasant things during life, how bitter it becomes in the last moments. For in proportion as they think the goods of the world are coming to them in ever-increasing abundance and at the same time they bind themselves all the more to them, so in that degree do they increase their own sorrows. The goods of the world seem openly good, but interiorly they are full of much evil. For this reason those who have a truly sane understanding should not become attached to that which proves itself to be only ephemeral.

At the end of this life, what usually happens? Think very seriously about this statement: "Of what profit is the world to those who have bound themselves to it?"[4] Even if one has much praise, honors, riches, are not all these as nothing? For is it not indeed like a passing shadow and as smoke that soon disappears?[5] And many of these men, immersed in and moved by the attractions of the things of this world, while enjoying youthful happiness, were harvested by death as flowers of the fields, in full bloom, cut down.[6] Even though they were unwilling, they had to depart from here. But when they were living yet in this world, they could not be bothered with reflection on its corrupting stench, but they busied themselves with beautifying the body and in seeking physical comforts. They were able to make their intellects apt for making worldly gains and they passed their time in studies, crowning the body in this fleeting time as the be-all and the end-all. Even if they attained all their desires, nevertheless, they could not be preoccupied about the future and unending happiness. What is to be thought of such persons? Are they not, as a certain wise saint said, the most foolish persons in the whole world?

Some of them, being more pious, turned their minds to thoughts about the desire to save their souls. They had the courage to wage war against the passions and live, as far as was possible, a virtuous life. They wanted to be freed and to cut themselves off from this world, but they were not able to detach themselves from its knot of snares and its evil cunning. The all-loving God has taken you from this world and placed you in his service by his mercy and design. For this you must give great thanks for his mercy and do all in your power to do all that will please him and that will serve for the salvation of your soul. Forget the past as not being profitable and strive for future virtue, which leads to eternal life.[7] Rejoicing, go on in the honor of such a noble calling which is bestowed upon those who seriously seek the heavenly *patria*. In regard to your question about impure thoughts which the devil implants in our souls, do not be too overwhelmed by this trial, nor be frightened. Because not only to us, so weak and passionate, does such opposition come, so the Fathers say, but also to those who have already progressed by a praiseworthy life and enjoy particular, spiritual graces; even they have a bitter struggle with such thoughts.[8] They undergo great fears of asceticism and by the grace of God barely manage to drive them away, being always conscientious to get rid of them. And you ought to be consoled by this, but carefully cut away all such evil temptations. Have at hand the constant, victorious prayer against them. Call on our Lord Jesus. With this cry you will drive away such thoughts which quickly enough will flee away, as John Climacus said: "Fight the enemy with the name of Jesus; there is no more powerful weapon."[9]

If these evil thoughts become more powerful in their attack against you, then rise up and with eyes toward Heaven and arms stretched out, sincerely say with compunction: "Have mercy on me, Lord, for I am weak.[10] You, Lord, are powerful and success is yours; fight for us and conquer, O Lord."[11] And if you will do so diligently with experience, you will learn in many ways how these thoughts are to be conquered by the power of the All-High. Do also some manual work, for such drives away evil thoughts. Such is the angelic tradition given to one of the great saints.[12] Learn something by heart from Holy Scripture. Concentrate your mind on this, for such passages turn back the onslaught of the devil. So have the Holy Fathers found it to be. Keep yourself from hearing conversations and seeing impure things for such stir up the passions and strengthen unclean thoughts.[13] God will help you.

You also mention fear. Fear is a trait of children and not for mature souls. But for you it should not have a place. When such thoughts occur, fight manfully so that they do not overcome you and make your heart resolute in a deep trust in God, saying the following: "I have a God who is watching over me. Without his will nobody can harm me in anything. Even if he allows something to happen to me which would make me suffer, I would not take that for evil, because I do not wish to make his will ineffective, because the Lord knows much more than I and wishes only my profit. So I am thankful for all because of his clemency." Thus with the grace of God, you will be firm in doing good. Arm yourself always with prayer and, when in whatever places such thoughts occur, be all the more careful in going there. Stretch out your hands in the form of a cross; call out to the Lord Jesus;[14] and, with the help of the Most High, do not be frightened "from the night's fear and from the arrows flying during the day."[15]

So much for these. In all other things as far as is praiseworthy, honorable, and virtuous, think about them and act; be courageous in good, hating all evil; give obedience to your superior and other Fathers in the Lord in regard to every good work. You have now been given a responsible position, or you will receive such a one. Fulfill it with brilliance and a devoted diligence, as serving Christ himself. Hold every brother as a saint.[16] If you must speak, ask a question, or give an answer to anyone, do it with a pleasant tone and gentle speech, showing spiritual love and true humility, and not an indifferent, superficial manner. Do not offend any brother. Stay close to a devout Father and this at the proper time and in the proper measure. Do not mingle with those who are not so. Keep yourself under control, not losing your temper. Do not judge anyone in anything, even if his actions appear not good, but consider yourself sinful and utterly useless. If from the superior or any other Father so appointed, you have need of anything, first pray over it, reflecting whether this is truly useful, and then ask for it. If a thing does not turn out as you would have wished, do not be dejected; no need to be angry simply because it did not turn out according to your wishing, even if a thing seemed good to you. But with patience go on and with calmness, and, taking your time, do all things. If you will so conduct yourself as to seek to please God and to save your soul, then God, knowing in all ways how to help and knowing also the exact time to do so for that end, will give you help according to your needs. Be sincerely bent on obeying the divine Writings. With their sayings your soul will be refreshed as with living water. Be careful as far as your strength permits to live according to them.

So to such as have an understanding of divine Writings and a spiritual wisdom and a life mirroring the virtues, to such, I say, strive to give yourself under obedience, and be an imitator of their way of life, showing patience in sorrows and praying for those who offend you. Consider those your benefactors. Understand that this which I am telling you is wisdom from divine Writings, which tell us the wish of God to do good. The saints of all times are those who "having served the cause of right, received the fulfillment of promises."[17] Those who walked in the paths of virtue not only bore hardships and sorrows, but even endured the cross and death and this is a sign of the love of God, that sufferings are granted to the one doing what is right. This is called a gift of God, according to the Apostle Paul in his writings. This has been given us from God, not only to believe in Christ, but also to suffer for him. This makes a man a participator in the passion of Christ,[18] and like to the saints who bore hardships for his Name. God blesses such in his Name who love him in no other way but by sending them temptations in the form of sufferings. And by this are the lovers of God distinguished from the others, that the first live in sorrows and hardships while the lovers of the world rejoice in food and comforts. And this is the true way, to bear trials of sufferings because of virtue. Teaching them to follow this path, God will lead his sufferers to eternal life.[19] For this reason it is becoming that we travel along this path with joy, keeping the commandments of the Lord and thanking him with all our heart for having sent us this blessing and grace out of his love for us. We must pray incessantly for his grace, recalling the end of this life of sorrows and the unending joy and consolation and these will keep you in his fear, by the prayers of the most pure Mother of God and all the saints. Do not forget me before the Lord. Remember me, a sinner, in your prayers, for I tell you what good you must do while I myself do not do it. May God deliver me from the swirling flood of passions and lead me out of the darkness of my sins.

LETTER II
OF THE SAME STARETS NIL
TO SOMEONE SEEKING HELP[20]

Even as in your pious conversation with me, most reverend Father, so also in your letter which you sent me, you ask me, so utterly incapable, to send you some useful written discourse, both pleasing to God and profitable to the soul. But I am a sinful man and unintelligent, overcome by every passion, and so I feared to begin such a thing. For this reason I have declined and put it off. But because your spiritual love orders me, even forces me beyond my capacity, to write you something edifying, for this reason I persuaded myself to do it.

Your first question: How to combat impure, carnal thoughts? About this not only must you have care and perform works of asceticism, but your whole being must fight the battle along with God, because this is a great struggle, the Fathers say, having a double conflict to wage in the soul as well as in the body. There is nothing more necessary for your very existence than this. For this reason one must be powerfully careful and diligent and courageous to keep one's heart from such thoughts. Having the fear of God before our eyes, we must remember our vows, which we have professed to live in chastity and purity. Chastity and purity not only look to external things of life, but also it means a man is chaste and pure when he protects his heart from polluting thoughts, by cutting out with great diligence all such thoughts. To gain this great victory over such thoughts it is necessary to pray to God. This was the constant tradition of the holy Fathers, expressed in various ways, but always the same thing understood. David is said to have prayed in this fashion: "My enemies now have surrounded me; my Joy, deliver me from those who have besieged me."[21] And another passage from his psalms says: "God, attend to my help,"[22] and others similar. Again another, "Judge, Lord, those insulting me and impede those who struggle against me,"[23] and other psalms. Call on the help of those about whose great exploits to preserve chastity and purity we read in their lives.[24] When the battle becomes very intense, then rise up and with eyes to Heaven and arms outstretched, pray thus: "You are powerful, O Lord, and yours is success. Fight on our behalf and be victorious in this battle, O Lord."[25] And cry out to the All-Powerful for help with the humble words: "Have mercy on me, Lord, for I am powerless."[26] For such is the teaching handed down by the saints. And if you will so conduct yourself in these struggles you will learn from experience, that by the grace of God, these (i.e., bad thoughts) are more easily conquered. "Always flog the enemies with the weapon of the name of Jesus,"[27] than which there is no more powerful way to attain victory. Keep yourself from seeing persons and hearing such conversations, for these stir up the passions and provide unclean thoughts and God will keep you from these.

In regard to your second question about blasphemous thought, this is indeed a shameless and cruel evil. It attacks with great force and at intervals. Such is not only the case now, but was also in ancient times. So the great Fathers and holy Martyrs found it and at the very moment when the tormentors wanted to inflict on their bodies wounds and bitter death, because they professed faith in our Lord Jesus Christ. And against this temptation they secured victory thus: They did not blame their own soul for this thought, but accused the wretched demon, saying against the blasphemous spirit: "Get behind me, Satan: I worship the Lord my God and him alone I serve."[28] "On you let your blasphemy be again heaped."[29] The Lord also writes thus: "Depart from me!"[30] "God who created me according to his image and likeness,[31] may he destroy you!" If after such a prayer the shameless thought still lingers on, turn your thought to something else, divine or human, if something proper can be found. Keep yourself from pride and take care to walk the path of humility. For the Fathers said: "Indeed, pride gives birth to blasphemous thoughts."[32] They happen out of the devil's envy for us. If from him or another source they come, like a deer bitten by a poisonous, wild beast, nevertheless, humility is capable of destroying this passion and not only this, but also others, so the holy Fathers said.[33]

In your third question you seek to know how to abandon the world and this shows your good diligence. Strive concretely to accomplish the following in your life, for this is the golden road to eternal life. Having understood in their clear wisdom, the blessed Fathers traveled along this way. For if one does not cut himself completely from the world, certain images and worldly habits, formerly acquired by him from hearing and seeing worldly things, again are renewed and one cannot carefully persist in prayer and learn to find always God's will. One wishing to learn how to please God must leave the world. Do not desire the pleasant conversations of your ordinary friends and of worldly wise men and of those absorbed in unending worries, such as the possessing of monastery wealth and properties, which they consider under the guise of generosity and from an ignorance of divine Writings, or from conducting themselves according to their own passionate ways which they consider virtues.[34] But you, O man of God, do not have anything to do with such. It is not fitting even to converse with such, not even to reprove or correct them, but let God do this, for God is powerful to correct them. Keep control of yourself in all ways with courageous boldness, for self-control is, as is written, like a great fire: "All things flee from its face" (Ex 14:25).

And turn away from hearing and seeing the affairs of the brethren and from their secrets and their actions. For that empties the soul of every good and makes one focus attention on the failings of the neighbor, while one leaves off weeping for his own sins. And do not be concerned to be engaged quickly in conversations with the brethren, even if they may appear to be helpful conversations. But if some brother wants to know something from us and truly seeks the word of God, and if we have something to give him, we even are obliged to give to him, not only the word of God, but according to the testimony of the Apostles, even our own soul. Give attention to such and wish them well in their labors, for they have spiritual wisdom and such are the children possessing the secrets of God. But conversations with others who are not of this type, even if few, tend to dry up the flowers of virtues. The garden of the soul, not long ago in full flower from the seclusion of *hesychia* and immersion in meekness and childlikeness, was planted by the flowing waters of penitence, as a wise saint said.[35]

In your fourth question you also ask how not to wander from the true path. About this I will give you good advice. Bind yourself to the laws of the divine Writings and follow them, the true Writings, divinely inspired. For there are many writings, but not all are divine. You, seeking the true from the various readings, stick to it and converse with prudent and spiritual men, because not all but only the intelligent understand these, and without proof from such writings, do not do anything. Thus have I always done.[36] See, your love for God makes me senseless even to the point of speaking about myself. But as it has been said: "My secrets I open to those who love me."[37] For this reason do I tell you this. For I do not act without testimony from the divine Writings, but finding something in them, I do it as far as in me lies. For when I must do something, first I search the divine Writings and if I do not find something in agreement with my understanding on how to begin a thing, I lay it aside until I do find something.[38] When I betake myself, by the grace of God, to the task, I do with tenacity that which is known. Of myself I do not dare to do such because I am an ignoramus and a peasant.[39] In this way, if you also wish, act according to the holy Writings and according to your understanding of them. Be diligent in keeping the commands of God and the tradition of the holy Fathers. And if the agitations of worldly things should disturb your heart, do not be alarmed. We rely on the unmovable rock of the Lord's commandments.[40] And we take defense by means of the traditions of the holy Fathers. Be zealous toward those whom you hear and see bearing witness by their living and wisdom to the same as is found in the holy Writings, for their way is the right way of journeying. And writing this deep in your heart, continue unswervingly in the way of the Lord and you will not err, by the grace of God, from the truth. For it is written that it is impossible for a wise man, knowing the right and living in virtue, to perish. But those who with a distorted mind do not do God's work transgress from the right path. Traveling without turning back, "having put your hand to the plow of the Lord and not looking back, you will be ushered into the Kingdom of God."[41] And take care that, having received the seed of the word of God, you do not turn your heart into a path of stone, nor thorns, but into fertile earth, bringing forth manifold fruit for the salvation of your soul.[42] Indeed, I rejoice, seeing your wisdom in hearing the word of God, and I praise worthily the things found in you and corrected by virtue. I give thanks to God, for I see in you one who, having heard the word of God, kept it. I beg you, for the sake of our Lord, pray for me a sinner, who preaches what good must be done, but does not do any of it myself. God, the Creator, praising exceedingly and giving in every way gifts to those who graciously do his will, may he give you intelligence and assurance to do his holy will, by the prayers of our most pure Queen, Mother of God, and all the saints, for he is blessed forever. Amen.

Letter III
of the Same Great Starets Nil
to a Brother Requesting Him to Write
Something of Profit to His Soul[43]

Your letter, Father, which you wrote me, requested me to write you something useful to you and at the same time to tell you something of myself. [You write] that you think I grieve because of the conversation which we had with you when you were still here. For this [you ask me] to pardon you. I give advice to myself and also to you as to my former, dear friend, recalling to the mind what is written: "I open my secrets to my sons of my house."[44]

We should not do things simply nor in a way only that seems best to us, but according to the divine Writings and according to the tradition of the holy Fathers. Before we left the monastery, was it not just for spiritual benefits and not for any other reason that we were guided in our actions? Nowadays one does not see in the monasteries an observance of the laws of God according to the holy Writings and the tradition of the holy Fathers, but rather we act according to our own wills and human ways of thinking and often we fall to the very seduction and do such things, all the while considering them acts of virtue.

This happens from our ignorance of holy Writings because we are not diligent to search the holy Writings with fear of God and humility, but in our carelessness we make them void by our human way of thinking. I spoke to you thus for this reason, because it is true, and because you are one who does not wish to hear and keep the word of God in a pharisaical manner. I, not pandering to you nor keeping from you the difficulty of the narrow and sorrow-ladened path, proposed to you a subject of this nature, but to others I speak in a different way about this same matter.

You know my utter incapability, right from the beginning, for you were my dear spiritual friend from the start. For that reason I now write you, speaking frankly about myself because your love for God forces me and makes me irrational even to the point of writing you about myself. When we lived in the monastery together,[45] you know how I removed myself from worldly enticements and how I have always acted as far as I have strength according to the divine Writings, even if I am incapable of that because of my laziness and ignorance. Thus, after I returned from my pilgrimage,[46] I came to the monastery, but I fixed for myself a cell outside and near the monastery and so I lived as far as my strength permitted. Now I have moved farther from the monastery, because, by the grace of God, I found a place suited to my thinking, where worldly people rarely come, as you yourself have seen. Chiefly, here I search the divine Writings, first the commandments of the Lord along with a commentary, and the apostolic traditions; then the lives and teachings of the holy Fathers. To these I attend, and what is in agreement with my understanding as to what would be pleasing to God and the good of my soul, I prescribe for myself. On such I meditate and in such I have my life and my very breath. But I abandoned all my inability and laziness and ignorance to God and the most pure Mother of God, and if it happens that I have something to do and if I do not find any solution in the holy Writings, I lay it aside for the time being until I do find [in them, i.e., the writings] something, because I do not dare to act according to my own will and intellect. And if anyone approaches me out of spiritual love, I also advise him in this manner, and above all, you, because from the very beginning you came to me out of spiritual love for advice. For this reason in preparing a discourse for you, I am advising you as to what good is to be done, as I would advise my own soul. As I myself am conscientious to do, so also I have spoken to you. If we are now physically separated, yet we are united by our spiritual love and we form a unity. As I then addressed you by way of explaining the monastery's rules with divine Love, so now I write you, seeking only your soul's salvation. And you, as you heard from me and as you yourself see in these writings, if there is something here that pleases you, should strive to be a son by imitation and an heir of the inheritance bequeathed by the holy Fathers. Keep the Lord's commands and the traditions of the holy Fathers. Tell also the brethren living with you. If you are alone in your cell (as a hermit), or in the monastery with the brethren, give your attention to the holy Writings and walk in the footsteps of the holy Fathers, because the divine Writings so command us. Or give yourself in obedience to the kind of person who will prove himself spiritual in thought, word, and deed. So St. Basil the Great wrote in one discourse which begins with the words "Come to me all you who labor."[47] If such a guide is not found, then give yourself in obedience directly to God through divine Writings and not so stupidly as some when they are in the monastery with the brethren and think they are obeying, yet they are fed inanely on their own self-will. They then leave and foolishly take up the anchoretic life, guiding themselves by their own carnal will and imprudent judgment. "For they know not what they do."[48] Those things apply to them as John Climacus says in his discourse on various kinds of "tranquillity": "There are some who out of conceit prefer to sail by their own discretion rather than under the guide and direction of another."[49] Let it not be so for us. But you, acting according to the holy Writings and the way the saints lived, by the grace of Christ, will not sin. Now I would be offended should you be sorrowful. For this very reason I was forced to write you, so you would not be so overwhelmed with sorrows. May the God of all joy and consolation console your heart and may he make known to you our love for you. If I have expressed this sentiment to you somewhat crudely, I did not wish to ignore your request. I hope that you will take this with charity and not look too much on my lack of intelligence. For our affairs and for those for which I begged your holy help, you have diligently and well arranged them, for which I am reverently grateful.

It was not [done] to any other, but to you, my beloved friend from so long ago. May God grant you a great reward for your labor.

Still I beg of your holiness one thing—that you do not take those words sorrowfully which I have spoken above. For if outwardly they seem harsh, they are nevertheless interiorly full of profit, because they are not my own words, but they have been taken from the holy Writings. They are truly harsh for those who do not wish sincerely to humble themselves in the fear of God and to abandon the false wisdom of the carnal world, but who insist on living according to their own passionate wills and not according to the holy Writings. Such do not search the holy Writings with spiritual humility. Some of them do not even wish these days to hear this, for they would say, "They were not written for us and it is impossible even for our present generation to observe them." But to the true laborers, in ancient and in present times and for all times, the words of the Lord are pure as purified silver and furbished seven times and his commands are illuminating and more desired than gold and precious gems. They please them better than honey and the honeycomb and they keep them. And they always will keep them and thus they will receive great rewards.

Greetings in the Lord, reverend Father, and pray for us sinners. We hold your sanctity in great respect.

LETTER IV[50]
FROM THE DIVINE WRITINGS OF THE FATHERS
TO A SUFFERING BROTHER[51]

For my brother in Christ, I, the least of our brethren, fulfill your request because I am forced from a sense of obligation to write and send to you that which I promised, so that you may know by means of that which I have written how much faith and love I have for you. I cannot bear, O my loved one,[52] to keep my secret in silence but I become foolish[53] and lose my head[54] when there is question of helping a brother, because this is true love: that one does not hide any secret from one's loved ones.[55] For a long time when I began to write these lines, my hand paused over the paper and I could not bear to move my sinful right hand without shedding sincere tears, recalling God's mercy and pity toward you. For he called you out of the land of Egypt,[56] and led you into the land of Israel and showed you the knowledge of our one, true God, Jesus Christ who became flesh. By his baptism you were baptized. Then he deemed you worthy to receive the angelic, monastic habit and with us you began your monastic life of the vows in our poor cell.

For this reason, brother, am I moved deeply in soul, perplexed in conscience, interiorly rent as I recall even from your youth your many sufferings and misfortunes, your imprisonment and exile from your native land of birth and from your *patria* to a strange and unknown land with a foreign language and there to live among illiterates and you, moreover, a son of most noble ancestors. How also the Lord delivered you in all these trials from many and diverse deaths; death from fire, sword, and water,[57] and he himself all the time had a better plan in mind for by these he led you to repentance and to a knowledge of the truth as God knows it. For this reason, namely, for our sins, has he inflicted on us temptations and sorrows and imprisonment. The Lord loves us and has mercy on us and wishes to instruct us with his wisdom by these trials. And I again rejoice in the fact that the Lord still so loves us, that not wishing to torture us in that future life, but here, he allows us to suffer in order to be purified from our sins. Thus I am going to write for love of you from the holy Writings to show you that the Lord sends these sorrows to those who love him and who are able to bear for his sake every sort of evil, for the Lord will never allow any evil to exceed our strength, according to the Apostle Paul.[58] And if he allows them, it is to be for the profit of the one tempted. But again and again for this reason, as was the case with those before us, all the saints of former times, prophets and apostles and martyrs were saved and are still being saved by sorrows, misfortunes, and persecutions. Let us recall first of all the just Job. Did he not rue the day he was born?[59]

Likewise Jeremiah the prophet said, "Woe is me; why was my mother ever born? Cursed be the night in which I was born."[60] And Moses, the great lawgiver of God, said, "Lord, if I ever found grace before you, take away my soul from me, for I cannot bear the burden of these people; rather would that they beat me with stones."[61] Habacuc the prophet complained: "Why did you send me labors and sicknesses?"[62]

Thus all the just suffered; the same is seen in the lives of the saints. May you model yourself on their example, because they were not fed during the time they lived their lives on any other than suffering such disturbing evils. What about the just David? Was he not persecuted all the days of his life, guarded, deprived of food? Did he not await death from Saul each hour in a strange land? Did not Abraham the just one suffer in a foreign land among infidels and barbarians and was his wife not snatched away from him? So also his son Isaac and his grandson Jacob. Even our Lord Jesus Christ, was he not led to the cross? Was he not pierced with a lance? Was he not buffeted in the face by slaps from the soldiers' hands? He was reckoned among criminals by the ungodly Jews. All these the Lord suffered for our salvation in order to free us from the oath of God.[63]

The earthly angel, John, the Lord's baptizer, did he not sit in prison? Did they not cut off his head with a sword? And then with tainted hands it was carried on a dish before the gluttonous feasters. O holy head, that looked on God and saw the Light of Dawn! O education in the desert from the cradle! Likewise the Prophet Elijah suffered much and was carried in a flaming chariot to Heaven. About the apostles, holy martyrs, our confessors and fathers, what is there to write?[64] They all suffered many and diverse deaths, misfortunes, slaying, and imprisonments for the sake of the heavenly Kingdom and all these in strange lands, among infidels and savage barbarians, preached the name of Christ. Some of them were crucified; some pierced by a lance; others given over to fire or the sword; others, tied with stones, were drowned in the sea; others devoured by beasts as food. And what more can we quote? Did they not rejoice in their sufferings of evils and sorrows? Joseph the fair, the son of the just Jacob of Israel and the favorite child of holy Rachel, was he not sold by his brothers into the bondage and service of his master Putiphar in the strange land of Egypt? I propose for you just one more account. Oh, what a terrible and fearsome fulfillment! I speak about the great orator and prophet Isaiah, who was put to death by the ungodly Jewish race by being cut in two by a wooden saw, right through his insides and his limbs, as if they were sawing through an inanimate log.

All suffered these abuses from infidel barbarians in strange lands for the Name of Christ. My brother, the all-seeing eye, God our Lord, foresaw you before your birth and loved you above all things, formed you from the womb of your mother, snatched you from the hellish mouths, from your own native land and beliefs, and brought you to a land to which you did not wish to go and did not even hope for such. He signed you with the seal of his Kingdom in the baptism of the Father and the Son and the Holy Spirit and adorned you as with a crown with the angelic habit. He led you to us to this unpopulated hermitage. He wishes you to suffer all sorrows, misfortunes, nakedness for the name of Christ and he allows such sorrows to befall us because he loves us, our Creator. "Whom the Lord loves, him will he chastise."[65] And if sorrows happen to us, greater than our being can support seemingly, let us rejoice in the hope of the future good. Let us strengthen one another, looking on all these saintly models and their lives and their achievements who have gone before us. What patient suffering for Christ as they poured out their very own blood! And if they, the just and holy, so suffered in whom the Holy Spirit dwelled and worked (for their miracles and great wonders we cannot sufficiently read through, nor describe them adequately), how much more it befits us to suffer for our innumerable sins. We ought not to become discouraged. But ought we not to strengthen one another to take courage in our mutual ascetical battle? The saints suffered for love of Christ. We should [at least] suffer for our sins. For this reason let us recall, O my favorite one, our crimes, as seen by our Creator, committed from our youth—how we have angered him; how we have violated his lifegiving commandments, and still how long he bears with us, waiting for our repentance and our return from our evil ways!

Recalling such mercy and unlimited forgiveness on the part of God, let us inflame our conscience. Let us pour out tears and sighs and similar acts of compunction. Henceforth with all strength let us not bother about carnal preoccupations, but present to God both our souls and bodies and let us diligently attend to the efficacy of the Name of the Lord in fighting temptations. Let us, with all our members, sail through them [the temptations]. Let us fill our eyes with spiritual tears and our hearts with deep sighs that accompany us to bed and arise with us in the morning. We have our guardian angel who will never forsake us. For this reason, God drives away the bitterness of these sorrows, not even allowing them to get near us. The enemy is weakened at the sight of our guardian angel protecting us. This God does for those loving him and those preparing themselves for death with great sincerity, for those who do not turn their backs to the enemy. Concerning this struggle and most bitter temptation, the child-loving Father, Isaac the Syrian, wishing to strengthen the weak souls, who take a wavering attitude toward asceticism, says the following: "Let there be among us that zeal in our souls against the devil and his helpers as the Maccabees and the holy prophets, apostles and martyrs, confessors and all the justified had. They suffered in their truth and were not filled with fear at such terrible sufferings surrounding their souls and bodies. But they conquered them manfully and put the devils' enticements and deceits behind them. Their stories and lives were written down as inspired and living models. How they endured, not yielding to the tender entreaties and allurements of evil-minded men, but with joy and sincerity they entered into the struggle with temptations and sorrows."

If it were not for sufferings, the Providence of God would not be seen as operative in mankind. It would be impossible to approach God with boldness; impossible to learn the wisdom of the Spirit and to be assured of the divine love in the soul. Before sufferings come to a person, he prays to God as if he himself were a stranger to him. But if he constantly struggles out of his love, soon he undergoes a change. Before, he held God as a taskmaster, but now he becomes a sincere friend of God. Do you see, brother, what a child-loving soul this heavenly Father [Isaac of Syria] possessed? Among his virtues he himself suffered and was tempted and thus he helps us in our temptations by strengthening our weak spirit and overcoming our incapability for asceticism, with the words of St. Paul, "For the present time of suffering will give way to future reward."[66]

Note, dear one, how pleasing to God is the prayer of a person suffering under temptations, according to the words of this amazing saint where he speaks above about a person holding God as a taskmaster, but when he has to bear sorrows, he becomes a sincere friend of God. Continuing, he [Isaac] says: "God does not bless those, even though they are chosen ones who honor him but still remain attached to carnal affections, but rather he blesses those who, as long as they were in the world, bore sorrows, difficulties, labors, deprivations, loneliness, lack of necessities, sicknesses and poverty, humiliations, insults, shame, harms from men and devils. They fostered sincere sorrow, harnessed the body, were cut off from compatriots and from their homeland and even from this earth. Thus they attained the wisdom of the compunction and embraced the monastic state and solitude, preferring the invisible world to the visible one of men.

"These weep, while the world laughs; these do penance while the world anoints itself with oil; these fast while the world seeks only pleasures. During the day they work and at night they devote themselves to asceticism in seclusion and in labors; some suffer with sicknesses; others in labors going against their passions; still others are persecuted by men; some in woes and sorrows produced by the devils and by other evil men; others are persecuted by them; some even beaten; others according to St. Paul 'experienced mockery and scourging, chains, too, and imprisonment; they were stoned, they were cut in pieces, they were tortured, they were put to the sword; they wandered about, dressed in sheepskins and goatskins, amidst want and distress and ill-usage; men whom the world was unworthy to contain, living a hunted life in desert and on mountain-sides, in rock-fastnesses and caverns underground.'"[67] The Lord knows how impossible it is to remain in his love in tranquillity as long as one is in this flesh and for this reason he prevents those enemies from disturbing his peace and sweet consolations. This God enjoins on those who love him and who wish to bear all evil for his name's sake. The word of God is fulfilled in them which says: "As you accept sorrows in this present life and do not become too enthralled by the world, for the world will hate you, know that it has hated me first."[68] Do you not see, O brother, that from former times all who ever were found pleasing to God reached salvation by means of sorrows and troubles and difficulties and entered into eternal joy? Of them it is written that the former type [those of this world] were powerful while the latter [the beloved of Christ] were weak and powerless.[69] About this the ancient skete Fathers prophesied that the last class would be called before the former because they pleased God more by their sorrows and misfortunes. See that God does not wish that those who love and honor him in this present life should have peace, and neither should the former type [persons of this world]. You, O lover of Christ, engrave all this on your heart and bear without weakening all sorrows.

Recall your initial faith at all times; your first fervor in undertaking the path of perfection, your ardent, burning thoughts with which you came to me in my poverty, in the uninhabited solitude, keeping solitary vigil and working only for my God from my youth. Recall also how you then were so careful about small transgressions even which you did not commit. It is the devil's wont, when he sees one beginning with an ardent faith to lead a good life, to make him suffer by various, passionate temptations, which arise from demons and from human beings, in order to bring him finally to fear. Having reached this weakness by means of suggested thought, the person destroys any good intention and never conceives in himself further the ardor to approach a harsh life full of suffering. And for these reasons, let us not weaken under these thoughts, but recall our sins from our youthful past, the terrible torments of hell for sinners and the rewards for the just. When we find ourselves strongly tempted, let us unflinchingly bear the temptations. A traveler, falling suddenly into such temptations, finds his liberation in the words of the Prophet: "Many sorrows befall the just and from all of them the Lord will deliver them,"[70] because they trust in him with every breath. "And they called to him and he heard them and protected them,"[71] and "he is with them in sorrows."[72] He delivers them and glorifies them and is their salvation according to his promise as he said, "I will not depart from you nor leave you."[73] He saved Joseph in Egypt and also Daniel, keeping him without harm in the den of the lions. The three youths in the blazing furnace also did not suffer harm. He delivered Jeremiah from the den of darkness and let Peter out of prison when the doors were closed. He saved Paul from the Jewish mob. Thus, in all this, the wonderful and merciful God, everywhere present and all-powerful, will direct us and free us if it be for the good of our souls. But only let us place all our hope and confidence and aspiration in him with all fervor. Let us bear as from the Lord these present gifts of sorrows, be they justified or unjustified; purified by them, we will stand without guilt before the judgment seat of Christ. To him praise and power forever and ever. Amen.

The Last Will and Testament[1]

In the name of the Father and of the Son and of the Holy Spirit I bequeath my last will and testament to my noble companions and brothers who are living the same moral life as I have lived.

I entreat you, cast my body out into the desert to be devoured by the wild animals and birds, since it has been the cause of my great sinning against God and is unworthy to be properly buried.

But if you do not do this, then dig a hole on the monastery grounds where we live and bury me with every kind of dishonor. Be fearful of these words which the great Arsenius enjoined as his last will and testament to his disciples, saying: "I will hold you accountable if you give over my body to anyone, for I have taken great efforts with all my strength so that no one would show me any fame and honor either in this life or after death."[2]

I beg all to pray for my sinful soul and I ask forgiveness from all as I forgive all. May God forgive us all.

I bequeath to my noble companions and brothers who will continue to labor in this monastery the large cross which contains the stone relic of the passion of our Lord, as well as the little books I have written. I would earnestly and with great humility implore that the holy service for the deceased be celebrated for me for the forty days after my death.

I also leave to them the small books of John Damascene, the book of prayers and the *Irmologion*.[3] The psalter copied by hand in quarto by Ignatius should be sent to the Kirillov Monastery. And all other books and objects which belong to that monastery which were given to me out of God's love should also be returned. For the rest distribute either to the poor or to some other monastery or to some needing Christian person. Let whatever of these be returned to their rightful owner.

Notes to the Introduction

1. *SGGD* (Sobranie Gosudarstvennyx Gramot i Dogovorov: Collection of Government Decrees and Treatises), 5 tomes (Moscow, 1813–1894), Vol. 2, no. 25, p. 27.

2. See E. Denisoff, "Aux Origines de l'Eglise Russe autocephale," in *Revue des Études Slaves* (1947), Vol. XXIII, pp. 66–88; W. K. Medlin, *Moscow and East Rome* (Geneva, 1952); and H. Schaeder, *Moskau das Dritte Rom*, Vol. 1 (Hamburg, 1929).

3. "Epistle of Joseph to Tret'yakov," cited by Ivan P. Kruschov, *Izsledovanie o sochineniyax Iosifa Sanina* (St. Petersburg, 1868), p. 226.

4. N. Barsukov, *Istochniki russkoi agiographii* (St. Petersburg, 1882), col. 406–407.

5. G. Maloney, *Russian Hesychasm* (The Hague-Paris: Mouton, 1973), p. 33, note 3.

6. Shchukin Moscow Museum, Ms. no. 212, seventeenth century, cited by M. S. Borovkova-Maikova, *Russkii Filogicheskii Vestnik*, Vol. LXIV (1910), pp. 61–64.

7. "Pis'mo o nelyubkax starstev Kirillova i Josifova monastryrya," in *Prib. k Tvor* (Pribavleniya k Tvoreniyam Svyatyx Otcev v russkom perevode), Vol. X, p. 505.

8. *Letter IV to Kassian, a Suffering Brother*; see Maloney, *Russian Hesychasm*, Appendix, p. 257.

9. The only other library richer was that of Troitska-Sergeeva Lavra, which had 300 manuscripts. Cf. N. Nikol'skii, *Materialy dlya povremennago spiska russkix pistatelei i ix sochinenii* (St. Petersburg, 1906), pp. XLV–XLVI.

10. Hesychasm is a Christian form of living the spiritual life that has its roots in the first hermits who fled into the barren

deserts of Egypt and Syria during the fourth century. It is a spiritual system of essentially contemplative orientation that finds the perfection of human beings in union with God through continuous prayer. This term is derived from the Greek word *hesychia*, which means tranquillity or peace. *Hesychia* is that state in which the Christian through grace and his or her own intense asceticism reintegrates one's whole being into a single person that is then placed completely under the direct influence of the Trinity dwelling within him or her. This present translation of Nil Sorsky's writings presents a vivid and practical overview of the elements of the ascetical and contemplative spirituality that goes by the name of hesychasm.

11. John Meyendorff, *Introduction a l'étude de Grégoire Palamas*, Vol. 3 in the collection *Patristica Sorbonensia* (Paris, 1959), p. 53.

12. "St. Nil was tonsured in the Kirill monastery from which he left and spent not a short time on the holy mount of Athos and in the regions around Constantinople." B. G. Grecev, "Prepodobnii Nil Sorskii i Zavolvskie Sta stsi," in *Bogoslovskii Vestnik* [1908], no. 2, p. 66, note 5. He cites this from a manuscript found in the Imperial Public Library, F. 1, no. 260, 1.56.

13. This hypothesis is suggested by A. Muravyev, *Russkaya Fevayda na severe* (St. Petersburg, 1894), p. 248.

14. We can hardly say that Nil was the first to have lived the skete type of monasticism in Russia. We know that it existed in the Novgorod region before Nil's time, but it never reached the Mt. Athos purity as found in Nil's skete and in his *Ustav* (*Rule*). Cf. I. Smolitsch, *Das russisches Mönchtum*, in *Das ostliche Christentum* 10/11 (Wurzburg, 1953).

15. For a complete description of the Athos model on which Nil based his skete, see P. Meyer, *Die Haupturkünden für die Geschichte der Athos-Klöster* (Leipzig, 1894).

16. The *Predanie* of Nil is his earliest attempt to give to his disciples a written, but very simplified, rule of skete monasticism. Borovkova-Maikova examined over 100 manuscripts found in Russian and found that 97 gave the *Predanie* and *Ustav* and 52 the letters of Nil. Her critical edition in old Slavonic of Nil's *Ustav* and *Predanie* is the basis for my translation. Unfortunately, we have no critical English edition of the letters.

17. The critical text of the *Predanie* and *Ustav* edited by Borovkova-Maikova and used in this translation is entitled *Nila Sorskago Predanie i Ustav s vstupitel'noi statei*, in *PDP* (*Pamyatniki drevnei pis'mennosti*), no. 179 (St. Petersburg, 1912).

18. Nil's *Ustav* is found on pp. 11–91 of the critical edition.

19. See note 17.

20. *Ustav*, p. 35 of critical edition.

21. *Predanie*, p. 2 of critical edition.

22. *Ustav*, p. 14 of critical edition.

23. Ibid., p. 14.

24. Cf. Nil Sinaite: "First we must fight the passions with much prudence which comes only through fighting. Then from our victories we can give to others of our conquests" (*PG* 28:835). Also *Vitae Patrum* (*PL* 22:857); Diadochus, *Capitula centum de perfectione spirituali* (*PG* 65:1167 ss.); Cassian, *Conferences*, ed. Dom. E. Pichery (Paris, 1935) in *Sources Chrétiénnes*, Vol. 4, chaps. 3 and 8, pp. 169, 173.

25. *Ustav*, p. 86 of critical edition.

26. *Ustav*, p. 16 of critical edition.

27. *Ustav*, pp. 39, 83 of critical edition. For a scholarly summary on the origins of the theory of the eight capital sins, see I. Hausherr, "L'origine de la théorie orientale des huit péchés capitaux," (*OC*) 30 (1933): 164–175.

28. Cf. Adnés, Pierre, "Hésychasm," in *Dictionnaire de Spiritualité* (*DS*) (Paris, 1969) Vol. 7, col. 384. See also I. Hausherr, "L'hésychasme: étude de spiritualité," (*OCP*) 22 (1956): 5–40 and 247–285; G. Maloney, *Prayer of the Heart* (Notre Dame, Ind., 1981).

29. Adnés, col. 384.

30. *Ustav*, pp. 82–83 of critical edition.

31. *Letter to German*, fol. 105A. Cf. Section 3: Letters of Nil.

32. *Letter to Gurii*, fol. 101A–B.

33. *Letter to Vassian*, fol. 97A.

34. *Ustav*, p. 81 of critical edition. Cf. Basil (*PG* 31:136B–C); and Climacus, *Ladder*, Step 27, (*PG* 88:1108C–D).

35. This is indeed Evagrius, *De Oratione* (*PG* 79:1169C). For the problem of Pseudo-Nil of Sinai, consult I. Hausherr, *Les léçons d'un contemplatif. Le Traité de l'oraison d'Evagre le Pontique* (Paris, 1960), pp. 5–8.

36. Hesychius, *Century* I (*PG* 93:1493D).

37. Nil follows Climacus closely in this teaching. Cf. *Ladder*, Step 27 (*PG* 88:1112A).

38. *Ustav*, p. 47 of critical edition.

39. Cf. Macarius (*PG* 34:905, 938 and following); and Nil Sinaite, *De Malignis Cogitationbus* 3 (*PG* 79:1204A–C).

40. Hausherr, "L'hésychasme," op. cit., p. 270.

41. *Ustav*, p. 28 of critical edition.

42. For a history of this word and various patristic descriptions, see Hausherr, "L'hésychasme," pp. 273–279.

43. Evagrius, *Practica* 50 (*PG* 40:1233B).

44. Philotheus, *De Mandatis* (*PG* 154:731B and following).

45. The best work on the subject of *penthos* is that of I. Hausherr, "Penthos," in *OCA*, no. 132 (Rome, 1944).

46. *Ustav*, p. 7 of critical edition.

47. Ibid., p. 77.

48. Ibid., p. 21.

49. Ibid., pp. 21–22. For a historical survey of how this formula evolved over the centuries, see I. Hausherr, *The Name of Jesus* (Kalamazoo, Mich., 1978); see also Maloney, *The Prayer of the Heart*.

50. Nil is quoting from the *Three Methods of Hesychastic Prayer*, which he wrongly attributes to Symeon the New Theologian (see *PG* 120:707B). For the true author of this work, see I. Hausherr, "Note sur l'invention de la méthode hésychaste," *OC* 20 (Rome, 1930): 180.

51. *Ustav*, pp. 14–15 of critical edition.

52. Ibid., p. 28.

53. See my translation of Symeon's *Hymns of Divine Love*, especially Hymn 13 (Denville, N.J.: Dimension Books 1975), pp. 44–46. On Symeon's mysticism see my, *The Mystic of Fire and Light* (Denville, N.J., 1975).

54. *Ustav*, p. 14 of critical edition.

55. For greater details on Nil's patristic sources, see Maloney, *Russian Hesychasm*, pp. 173–198.

56. A. S. Orlov, "Iisusova molitva na Rusi v 16 veke," *PDP* (1914), p. 18.

57. *Apatheia* is the Greek word the patristic, hesychastic Fathers

used to describe the goal of all *praxis* or their ascetical practices. Although it has its roots and received much influence from the Stoic concept, the Christian writers never considered human passions evil. One could not take the first step in sanctity if he or she did not have the desire to love God and a certain basic fear of sin. After grace filters down into one's heart and true love conquers the heart, *apatheia* results in the state of integration and the goal of divinization for which God created human beings in his own image and likeness.

58. For the main elements of the Macarian school of spirituality, see G. A. Maloney, *The Writings of Pseudo-Macarius* (Mahwah, N. J.: Paulist Press, 1992).

59. See J. S. Lur'e, *Ideologicheskaya bor'ba v russkoi publitchistike konsa XV -nachala XVI veka* (Ideological Struggle in Russian Polemical Literature at the End of the 15th and the Beginning of the 16th Century) (Moscow, 1960), pp. 285–296.

60. An example of oversimplification can be found in E. Behr-Sigel, *Priére et Sainteté dans l'Eglise russe*, in *Collection Russie et Chrétienté* (Paris, 1950), Ch. 6, pp. 76–88. Cf. G. Fedotov, *Sviatye Drevnei Rusi* (Paris, 1931), pp. 166–175.

61. Cf.: pp. 5–6 of Introduction.

62. Feb. 1489, "Letter of Archbishop Gennady to Ioasaf, Archbishop of Rostov," in Manuscript of Troiskaya Lavra, no. 730, fol. 246 ff., now found in the Lenin Library in Moscow.

63. "Pis'mo o nelyubkax starstev Kirillova-Iosifova monastyrya," ed. I. Panov, in *Otnosheniya inokov Kirillova i Iosifova monastyrey*, in *Prib. k Tvor.*, T. X, p. 505.

64. See the classic work on this subject, A. S. Pavlov, *Istoricheskii otcherk seculyarizasii cerkovnyx zemel' v Rossii.* Part I: *Popytki k obrascheniyu v gosudarstvennuyu sobstvennost' pozemel'nyx vladenii russkoi cerkvi v XVI veke (1503–80)* (Odessa, 1871), ed. Zapiski Novorossiiskogo Universiteta; Part V; Vol. VIII, 18.

65. Vassian was sent on a mission along with other boyar leaders, including the Josephian denounced heretic, Iva Kurcyn, along with Vasily and Simeon Ryapolovsky to arrange the marriage of Ivan III's daughter Helene to Alexander, Grand Prince of Lithuania. Cf. *PSRL*, Vol. IV, 164; VI, 39, 240; VIII, 228.

66. *Prav. Sob.*, III (1863): 203.
67. Cf. *Russian Hesychasm*, op. cit. *RH*, pp. 37–69.
68. "Nil Sorsky i Paisy Velitchkovsky," *Collection dedicated to S. F. Platonov* (St. Petersburg, 1911), pp. 27–31.
69. Ibid., p. 32.
70. *Zitie i tvorieniya prepodobnago i bogonosnago otsa nashego Nila Sorskago* (Life and Compositions of Our Saintly and God-bearing Father Nil Sorsky). But curiously no mention is made that this is the work of Bishop Justin. The two editions of his work with the same title, that I could check (Moscow, 1892, and Berlin, 1939) are identical with this new edition of 1958. In presenting Nil's *Ustav*, the author gives substantially the whole composition, but it was not meant to be a literal translation.
71. Ibid., p. 6.

Notes to the Text

The Tradition (*Predanie*)

1. In the Ms. 142 (16–17th cent.), a Rumanian manuscript found in the Moscow Museum in the Indilsky Collection, we learn that Nil Sorsky is identified as a hermit living the skete style of monasticism in the Sorsky hermitage in the Greater Russia, which was connected with the large coenobitic monastery of the most holy Birth-Giver of God of Kirill Monastery.

2. St. John Climacus is famous as the author of *The Ladder of Paradise*, a classical treatise of Eastern Christian asceticism that he divides into thirty chapters of steps of a ladder to perfection. He was an abbot of St. Catherine's Monastery in Sinai in the seventh century.

3. St. Maximus is one of the outstanding mystics and theologians of the Eastern Christian Churches (580–662). After a career in civil service, he became a monk around 614 in the monastery of Philippikos in Chrysopolis (Scrutari, close to Constantinople). He was a leader in opposing the Christological heresies of Monoenergism and Monotheletism and was sent into exile.

4. 2 Thes 3:10.

5. Mt 5:40.

6. Basil the Great (330–379) is the Father of Greek monasticism whose so-called *Rules* are actually spiritual counsels.

7. St. Barsanuphius was an Egyptian by birth. He lived in the sixth century, mostly in Palestine, and was famous for his life of strict silence without any contact with other human beings for some thirty years. He died in 563. He wrote on the gift of tears and the heremitical life and enjoyed the gift of clairvoyance and prophecy.

8. St. Isaac of Nineveh was a seventh-century Syrian monk whose ascetical and mystical writings were very popular.

9. St. Dorotheus lived at the end of the sixth and the beginning of the seventh centuries. He was trained by SS. Barsanuphius and John in monasticism and became an abbot in Palestine. His homilies to his disciples, *Directions on Spiritual Training*, and a few letters are all we have of his writings.

10. St. John Chrysostom (meaning the Golden-Mouth), was born in Antioch c. 347 of wealthy parents and was well educated in the Greek classical manner. Baptized at the age of eighteen, he withdrew into solitude in the desert and there, through his severe mortifications, ruined his health. Returning to Antioch, he prepared for ordination to the priesthood and began a long life of preaching against the paganism found in the cities of Antioch and Constantinople, where he had been elevated to Archbishop and Patriarch respectively. His volumes of commentaries on the books of the Bible and his homilies became the source of much of the reading among the Slav Christians, especially of the clergy and monks of Russia. He died in 407 in exile because of his outspoken sermons against the wife of the Emperor, Eudoxia.

11. St. Eugenia was martyred under Emperor Commodus (180–192) and was buried in the Catacombs of the Appian Way. Her feast day is celebrated in the Christian East on December 24.

12. St. Pachomius is the famous founder of coenobitic monastic communities in Egypt. Tradition tells us he received his monastic rule, the first for coenobitic communities, from an angel. He died †348.

THE MONASTIC RULE (*Ustav*)

1. Mt 23:26; Jn 4:23.
2. 1 Cor 14:19.
3. Barsanuphius the Great, "Directions in Spiritual Work," in *Writings from the Philokalia on "Prayer of the Heart,"* tr. E. Kadloubovsky and G. E. H. Palmer, no. 96–99, pp. 370–371.

4. St. Isaac of Nineveh wrote many works on asceticism and mysticism in Syriac and Arabic. He entered the monastery of St. Matthew near Nineveh and spent several years in solitude. He was consecrated bishop of Nineveh, but after a few years he returned to his solitary life in the desert. He relied much on the writings of Evagrius but went further in describing a superior state of continual prayer that he called "pure prayer." Isaac wrote much on the importance of the gift of tears.

5. Philotheus of Sinai was abbot of the monastery of Mt. Sinai. His most famous work is *Forty Texts on Sobriety*. The dates of his birth and death are not known.

6. For an explanation of the concept of *apatheia*, cf. note 57, page 38 of the Introduction.

7. Symeon the Studite, the spiritual elder of St. Symeon the New Theologian, was a simple monk, not a priest. He is called "the Studite" because he lived in the Monastery of the Studion in Constantinople in the tenth century.

8. St. Gregory of Sinai was first tonsured a monk in the monastery of Mt. Sinai in the fourteenth century and hence is called "the Sinaite." He went to Mt. Athos and began a revival of hesychasm with special accent on the method of praying the Jesus Prayer. Cf.: *Writings from the Philokalia on "Prayer of the Heart,"* pp. 35–94, for some excerpts of his writings.

9. For an explanation of the spirituality called "hesychasm," cf. note 28 of the Introduction.

10. St. Hesychius was born in Jerusalem and was a monk before accepting ordination to the priesthood. He is celebrated in the Christian East as one of the great teachers of the spiritual life and a noted preacher as well as exegete of Holy Scripture.

11. "Being sober" is called *nepsis* in Eastern Christian spirituality. It comes from the Greek verb *nepo*—I am sober and not intoxicated.

12. These psychological stages of the development of thoughts that lead to sin and vice are taken from St. John Climacus. Cf. *Ladder*, Step 15 (*PG* 88:896D). See Maloney, *Russian Hesychasm*, p. 79, for other Fathers who similarly depended on Climacus and used his divisions.

13. Peter Damascene does not mean passions as the same as our natural emotions, but rather he means the irascible and concupiscible passions under the power of sin that leads away from *apatheia* or reintegration with God's grace to the world of disharmony and captivity to sin. Peter's life is not well known, except from the details of his vast writings. He lived in the twelfth century. His writings deal mostly with the personal asceticism and prayer of the individual hesychast.

14. Nilus of Sinai belonged to a wealthy family and was a pupil of St. John Chrysostom when the latter preached in Antioch. Married and father of two children, he settled in the monastery of Mt. Sinai with his son, while his wife and daughter entered Egyptian convents. He and his son lived in a cave in the wilderness of Sinai and there Nil wrote his very popular treatises on the spiritual life. He died in 450.

15. Hesychius of Jerusalem (see note 10) was a pupil of St. Gregory the Theologian and became famous for his learned writings, preaching, and interpretation of Holy Scripture. He died in the year 433.

16. Cf. note 8. For an English translation of a Russian classic on the Jesus Prayer through the teachings of the Fathers of the *Philokalia*, see R. M. French, *The Way of a Pilgrim* (London, 1930).

17. Here Nil attributes the well-known classic on the three methods of hesychastic prayer, tied to the traditional Jesus Prayer, to Symeon the New Theologian. But cf.: I. Hausherr, op. cit. (see Bibliography).

18. Nil often uses as in this case the Slavic word *bezmolviye* to translate the word in Greek of the Greek Fathers, *hesychia* ("inner tranquillity").

19. Nil deals with acedia as number 6 of the eight principal vices or "passionate" thoughts that are the root of all sin in this chapter, no. 6 in part 5. In general Nil gives no precise definition nor even a description, as Cassian and Climacus do. He presupposes each monk has had personal experience of the temptation and its terrible effects. He fears this vice of depression and dejection that fills the monk with great doubt about his style of life and the desire to leave the monastic state, yet he also insists that nothing

furthers a monk's perfection in grace so much as this spiritual "dark night" of the soul. Cf. *Ustav*, p. 52.

20. *Tropars* refers to certain liturgical hymns chanted in the Eastern Churches' liturgies and Office.

21. The "Trisagion" refers to a hymnal prayer often repeated in the liturgies and Offices of the Christian East. It reads: "Holy God, Holy Almighty One, Holy Immortal One, have mercy on us." It refers to the thrice-holy Trinity, Father, Son, and Spirit.

22. St. Macarius has been falsely claimed as the author of the Macarian Corpus, especially the homilies of Macarius. He was born in Upper Egypt and entered the desert of Scetis and there lived as a hermit for sixty years. He was famous for his unusual gifts of spiritual direction and discernment and the gifts of healing and prophecy. Today scholars have proved that the real author of the Macarian Corpus was an anonymous fourth-century Syrian of Mesopotamia. See Maloney *Pseudo-Macarius: The Fifty Spiritual Homilies and the Great Letter*, in *The Classics of Western Spirituality* (Mahwah, N. J.: Paulist Press, 1992).

23. St. Anthony the Great is considered the father of Christian monasticism and the first Christian hermit. He was born of Christian parents about 250 at Coma in Middle Egypt. As a young man he sold all his belongings and gave the money to the poor and practiced the ascetic life not far from his home. He died at the age of 105 in 356 on Mt. Colzim near the Red Sea. St. Athanasius wrote his famous *Vita* of Anthony, which became a model of hagiography throughout the history of monasticism.

24. On acedia, see note 19. No. 6 in list, part 5.

25. Nil refers often to the common teaching of the early Fathers of the hesychastic tradition on *nepsis*. This word comes from the Greek *nepo*, which means not to be intoxicated. The true Christian must be interiorly attentive to the inner movements of the "heart" by guarding the mind and the heart by vigilance. One is not to be intoxicated by the things of this world, but to be "sober" and vigilant over every thought, word, and deed.

26. When Nil refers to "passions," he does not mean the basic emotions, such as our irascible and concupiscible emotions that are

a part of God's creation of us as human beings. He refers always to the basically good constitutive parts of a human being, but now as they are under the dominion of sin and death. In this situation a person lives in slavery to his carnal-mindedness and not according to one's true self, guided by the Holy Spirit.

27. The catalogue of the eight principal vices or passions first appears in the writings of Evagrius, Nilus of Sinai, and John Cassian. See I. Hausherr, "L'origine de la théorie orientale des huit péchés capitaux," *OC* 30 (1933): 164–175.

28. *Ustav*, p. 40. Nil is evidently paraphrasing Cassian's teaching. See *Conférences* 54 (*Sources Chrétiénnes* 42, pp. 190–191).

29. Cf. *Dobrotolybie*, ed. Bishop Theophan the Recluse (Moscow, 1884), Vol. 2 (1884), no. 30, p. 60.

30. According to the Greco-Roman system for calculating the time of day and night, the day from sunrise to sunset was divided into twelve hours with a period longer in summer, shorter in winter. The ninth hour corresponds to our 3:00 P.M.

31. St. Basil, *Long Rule* (*PG* 31:969A).

32. See Cassian, *De Institutis Coenobiorum*; as edited by M. Petschenig, *Corpus Scriptorum Ecclesiasticorum Latinorum* (*CSEL*) (Prague-Vienna, 1838), Book VI, 1, p. 115.

33. Climacus, *Ladder*, Step 15 (*PG* 88:879D).

34. Isaac the Syrian, *Logos* 54 (*PG* 86A:320).

35. Nil depends greatly on Cassian in dealing with covetousness. See *De Institutis Coenobiorum* 7 (*CSEL* 17:130–149).

36. Ibid., 8.11 (*CSEL* 17:158).

37. Dorotheus (*PG* 88:1714C).

38. See Isaac in *PG* 86:817C–D; 852D; 853A.

39. See Gregory Sinaite, *Chapters* (*PG* 150:1279C).

40. St. Basil, *Long Rule* (*PG* 31:1368A).

41. Nil copies this text from Gregory Sinaite, *Chapters* (*PG* 150:1279C–D).

42. Cf. Isaac, *Logos* (*PG* 86:851C–D).

43. Cf. Climacus, *Ladder*, Step 23 (*PG* 88:970D).

44. On this point, see also Dorotheus, *Doctrina* 10 (*PG* 88: 1724D).

45. Isaac the Syrian, *Logos* 39 (*PG* 86:248).

46. *Ustav*, pp. 66–67. The ideas and language used here are similar to those found in the penitential canons sung in the Byzantine-Slav Church in various Lenten Offices.

47. *Ustav*, pp. 70–71. Although Nil does not hint as to his source for this prayer, there are common elements found in the prayer of the martyr St. Eustratius, *Vita*, chap. 32 (*PG* 116:505B–C), and in a prayer given in the life of St. Macrina, written by her brother, St. Gregory of Nyssa (*PG* 46:984C–985A).

48. Climacus, *Ladder*, Step 7 (*PG* 88:816B).

49. Nil here is quoting in general the teaching of Gregory of Sinai found in *PG* 150:1326A.

50. Cf. Symeon the New Theologian, (*PG* 31:1368A).

51. For a similar teaching, see Isaac the Syrian in *Dobrotolubie*, Vol. 2, pp. 754–755.

52. See Jos 15:18–19. This text of St. Pope Gregory the Great is found in *PL* 77:819–880B (*Epistola ad Theoctistam*).

53. Cf. 2 Cor 3:5.

54. St. Andrew, Archbishop of Crete, composed in the twelfth century a famous penitential canon, a collection of hymns and prayers arranged around a given theme. (There are liturgical canons for Matins, canons for private devotions to the Mother of God, and for individual saints and angels.) Andrew's canon of repentance is sung during the Lenten period in most Byzantine churches.

55. St. Ephrem the Syrian, *Sermo Asceticus* (ed. Assemani), Vol. 1, p. 61.

56. St. Symeon the New Theologian, *Capita Moralia* (*PG* 31:640D, 645B, 517D).

57. *Troparia* (*tropar*, sing.) are hymns sung in the Byzantine Liturgy and the Divine Office, similar to the Collects used in the Roman Rite.

58. Cf. Climacus, *Ladder*, Step 7 (*PG* 88:808C; also 805D).

59. Ibid., Step 7 (816B). See Hausherr, *Penthos*; in *OCA*, no. 132 (1955).

60. Isaac the Syrian, *Logos* 75 (*PG* 86:503).

61. Nil no doubt is referring to the clash between him and his Transvolgian hermits in their strict practice of poverty against

Joseph Volokalamsk and his coenobitic monks who owned large farms and much property outside the monastery.

62. The *Paterikons* were collections of selected writings of the early Fathers of the desert, usually by anonymous editors. When manuscripts were rare of the full texts of certain Fathers, the *Paterikons* gave selections chosen according to themes.

63. No doubt Nil is quoting from St. Basil, who pointed out the dangers of the strict, solitary life of hermits as well as those who lived the coenobitic life. The "golden mean" was for Basil and Nil the skete life.

The Letters

1. This letter is addressed to the Prince-monk Vassian Patrikeev. I follow in this translation the Troitsky-Sergeivy Ms. 188, fol. 93–98, now found in the Lenin Library in Moscow.

2. Archbishop Philaret Kar'kovskii in his *Obzor russkoi duchovnoi literatury* (*Survey of Russian Spiritual Literature*) (Karkov, 1859), in note 116, claims this letter was sent by Nil to the Prince-monk Kassian Mavnukskii and many subsequent authors repeat this opinion. But I hold with Gorsky, "Otnosheniya inokov Kirillova-Belozerskago i Iosifova-Volokolamskago monastirei v XVI veke," *Prib.k Tvor.*, 10 (1851), p. 502, and A. S. Archangelskii, *Nil Sorskii i Vassian . . .* , *PDP*, no. 25 (St. Petersburg, 1882), p. 58, on the basis of this Troitskii Ms. 188, which I have had access to, that it was addressed to Vassian as can be seen from the top of fol. 93.

3. Surely a sign of Nil's self-abasement and not an indication that he was of a peasant class and not well educated.

4. Mt 16:26.

5. Wis 2:2–5.

6. Ps 102:15.

7. Ph 3:13.

8. *Ustav*, p. 34.

9. Climacus, *Ladder*, Step 21 (*PG* 88:945C); *Ustav*, p. 23.

10. Climacus, *Ladder*, Step 15 (900D); *Letter to Gurii*, Vol. 100.

11. Already quoted in Nil's earlier letter to Gurii, fol. 100, where Nil takes his citation from Isaac, *Logos* 54.

12. *Ustav*, pp. 32–33, where Nil quotes the tradition as given in the *Vita S. Antonii* (*PG* 65:76A–B).

13. Advice given also to Gurii, fol. 102.

14. Climacus, *Ladder*, Step 15 (900D).

15. Ps 90:5.

16. Probably Nil is here quoting from Symeon the New Theologian, who has the same thought (*PG* 120:669D).

17. Heb 11:33.

18. 2 Cor 1:5.

19. 1 Cor 1:18 and following.

20. Letter written to Gurii Tushin. Again in the Troitsky Ms. no. 188, there is written on top by hand the name of the receiver: "Gurii Tush" (fol. 99A). He was a nobleman of the Kvashnin-Tushin family, son of the boyar Michael Aleksandrovitch. Bishop Amvrosii in his listing of the higoumens (superiors of a monastery) of the Kirill-Belozerskii Monastery indicates Gurii as the tenth after the founder, of St. Kirill. He held office in 1461–1462 for nine months. Cf. *Istoriya rossiiskoi Ierarchii Sobrannaya byvshim novgorodskoi Seminarii prefektom Ep. Amvrosiem* (Moscow), *IRI*, Vol. IV, p. 497. Gurii enjoyed a reputation as a spiritual director and also followed Nil's example in the literary editing of *Lives of the Saints*. He died July 8, 1526.

21. Ps 107:13–19.

22. Ps 22:19; 40:13; 7:12.

23. Ps 31:17; 35:1, 22, and following.

24. *Ustav*, p. 44.

25. Nil already quoted this from Isaac the Syrian in his *Ustav* in treating the vice of fornication, p. 45. See Isaac, *Logos* 54.

26. Ps 6:3; Climacus, *Ladder*, Step 15 (*PG* 88:900D).

27. Climacus, *Ladder*, Step 21 (945C).

28. Mt 4:10.

29. Ps 7:17; Climacus, *Ladder*, Step 23 (977B–C).

30. Mt 16:23.

31. Gn 1:26.

32. Climacus, *Ladder*, Step 23 (965C; 969B–C; 976B–C).

33. Ibid., Step 25 (1004A).

34. A clear reference to Joseph and his school of followers.

35. Gregory Sinaite (*PG* 150:1333D), but Gregory is evidently also borrowing from Climacus, *Ladder*, Step 28 (1129B).

36. Nil repeats in this paragraph exactly what he had said to German. Cf. 105B.

37. Letter to German, 104A.

38. Ibid., 105B–106A.

39. *Poslyanin* in the Slavonic. For this reason Arxangel'skii and Grečev believed Nil to have been of the peasant class, but it is evidently an expression of his self-abasement and humility.

40. 1 Cor 10:4.

41. Lk 9:62.

42. Lk 8:5 and following; Mk 4:26 and following.

43. I follow again the Troitskii Ms. no. 188, fol. 104–108, now in the Lenin Public Library. It is found also, as the other letters of Nil, in an uncritical edition by Elagin. I place it here as the third of Nil's letters because this is the order found in Ms. 188 used for my translation. From the content it is clear, however, that it was written shortly after Nil's arrival back from the East, for he mentions his withdrawal from the Kirill-Belozerskii Monastery as a recent event. It is written to Starets German Podol'nii, as the manuscript indicates. German was of noble birth and entered the Kirill-Belozerskii Monastery. He was also in the Podol'nii Monastery in 1509–1510, from which monastery he gets his last name. He was probably living a hermit's type of life. German died April 30, 1533.

44. Cf. Jn 17:26.

45. This is the Kirill-Belozerskii Monastery where Nil was first tonsured, and, as we learn in this letter, to which he returned after his pilgrimage to the East.

46. The only manuscript giving any authentic biographical data about Nil is Ms. 212, found in the Shchukin Moscow Museum (seventeenth century), cited by Borovkova-Maikova, in "Velikii Starets Nil, Pystynnik Sorsky," *Russkii Filogicheskii Vestnik*, Vol. 64 (1910): 62–64.

47. The manuscript at this point is not clear and I was unable to locate this composition of St. Basil. Passages similar to this are

found in Basil, *Ep. 188* 15–16 (*PG* 32:681C–684B); *Ep. 204* (*PG* 34:744–756); and *Hom. in Princ. Prov.* 8 (*PG* 31:404A).

48. Lk 23:24.

49. Climacus, *Ladder*, Step 27 (1105A).

50. Letter to Kassian. I am following in this translation Ms. 185, fol. 363–375, earlier found in the Moscow Ecclesiastical Academy and now in the Lenin Library. This is the longest letter by Nil that we have. Due to the subject matter, it reveals better than any other of his works Nil's literary style plus his intimate knowledge of St. Paul.

51. Kassian, before becoming a monk, was Prince Konstantin Mavnukskii, who came to Russia in the cortege of Sophia Paleologue. He was born in Amorea, was friendly with the Russian hierarchy, and was in the service of Archbishop of Rostov, Ioasaf. Ioasaf was stripped of his office in a clash with Ivan III. With him fell also Prince Konstantin, who was forced against his will to be tonsured in the Ferapont Monastery near Nil Sorsky's hermitage, taking the name of Kassian. He died October 2, 1504, and is honored on the same day as a saint.

52. *Lubimche moi*, which indicates the intimate, personal warmth that permeates Nil's letters and that is so absent from the strictly "patristic" teachings in his *Ustav*.

53. *Bezumen* in Slavonic.

54. *Jurod* in Slavonic.

55. Jn 14:21. See also the Letter to German, 104A.

56. Hos 11:1; Mt 2:15.

57. Heb 11:34.

58. 1 Cor 10:13.

59. Jb 3:3.

60. Jer 20:14.

61. Num 11:11.

62. Hab 1:3.

63. Gal 3:13.

64. Heb 11:32 and following.

65. Heb 12:6; 1 Cor 11:32; Rev 3:19.

66. Rom 8:18.

67. Heb 11:36.

68. Jn 15:18.
69. 1 Cor 1:18 and following.
70. Ps 34:19–20.
71. Ps 107:6, 13.
72. Ps 33:18; 34:18–21.
73. Heb 13:5; Ps 117:6.

THE LAST WILL AND TESTAMENT

1. I translate Nil's Last Will and Testament from the critical edition of M. S. Borovkova-Maikova, where this text is found on p. 10. I also was able to check her text when I worked on Ms. no. 188, formerly in the library of the Troitsky-Sergieva Lavra, but now found in the Lenin Library of Manuscripts in Moscow.

2. This passage is based on no. 40 of the sayings of Arsenius in the "Alphabetical Collection" of *The Sayings of the Desert Fathers*, tr. Benedicta Ward, SLG (Kalamazoo, Mich.: Cistercian Studies Series; 1984); no. 40, p. 18. Cf.: *PG 65*, col. 105B.

3. The *Irmologion* is a liturgical book containing hymns and prayers for various liturgical services that are usually sung and not read.

A Selected Bibliography

A. Editions of Nil Sorsky's Writings Consulted

Akty Instoricheskie. St. Petersburg, 1841.

Borovkova-Maikova, M. A. "Nila Sorskago Predanie i Ustav s vstupitel'noj statej." *PDP*, no. 179. St. Petersburg, 1912.

Dobrotoljubie, Ed. *Bishop Theophan the Recluse.* Tome I, 1895; Tome II, 1884; Tome III, ed. 2 & 3, 1888; Tome IV, 1889; Tome V, 1889.

Elagin Edition. "Prepodobnyj Nil Sorskii pervoosnovatel' skitskago zhitija v rossii, i ustav ego o zhitel'stve skitskom." St. Petersburg, 1864.

Justin Episkop. *Prepodobnyi i bogonosnyj otec nash Nil, podvishnik Sorsky.* Moscow, 1892; Berlin, 1939; Toronto, 1958.

Lenin Library of Moscow. Manuscripts of Nil's letters: a. Letter to Vassian Patrikeev, Troick. Ms. no. 188, fol. 93–98; b. Letter to Gurii Tushin, Ms. no. 188, fol. 99–103; c. Letter to German Podol'nyi, Ms. no. 188, fol. 104–108; d. Letter to Kassian Mavnuksky, Moscow Ecclesiastical Seminary, no. 185, fol. 363–375; e. Letter to a Brother in an Eastern Country, Volokalamsk Ms., 189/577, fol. 22–23.

Synodal edition. *Prepodobnogo otca nashego Nila Sorskago predanie uchenikom svoim of zhitel'stve skitskom.* St. Petersburg, 1852.

156

Fedotov, G. *Svjatye drevnej rusi.* Paris, 1931.

Lilienfeld, Fairy von. *Nil Sorsky und seine schriften—die krise der traditionim russland Ivans III, II teil: Die schriften Nil Sorskys in deutscher ubertragung.* Berlin, 1963.

B. RELATED SOURCES CONSULTED

Akty Arxeograficheskoj Komissii. St. Petersburg, 1836 & following.

Drevnerossijskaja Biblioteka. 2nd ed. Moscow, 1788–1791.

Gennadij, Bishop of Novgorod. "Letter to Ioasaf." Troickaja-Lavra Ms. no. 730, fol. 246, reproduced by Kazakova-Lure. In *Antifeodal'nye ereticheskie dvizhenija na rusi XIV nachala XVI* v. no. 16, pp. 315–320. Moscow, 1955.

Isaac the Syrian. *De perfectione religiosa.* Edited by P. Bedjan. Paris, 1909.

Izdanie obshchestva ljubitel'nej drevnej pis'mennosti. St. Petersburg, 1878–1911.

Kurbsky, Prince. "Poslanie Kurbskago." *Prav. sob.,* June 1863, pp. 571ff.

Pamjatniki drevnej pis'mennosti (PDP). St. Petersburg, 1816–1925.

Patrologiae cursus completus, series Graeca (PG). Edited by J. P. Migne. Paris.

Patrologiae cursus completus, series Latina (PL). Edited by J. P. Migne. Paris.

Polnoe sobranie russkix letopisej (PSRL). St. Petersburg, 1841 & following.

Russkaja istroicheskaja biblioteka (RIB). Izd. Arxeograficheskoj Komissii. St. Petersburg, 1879 & following.

Sobranie gosudarstvennyx gramot i dogovorov. 5 tomes. Moscow, 1813–1894.

Stoglav. 3rd ed. Kazan', 1911.

Trans Volga Starcy. "Letter of the Trans-Volga Starcy." ms. ed. Kazak.-Lur'e. *DRB*, Vol. XVI, pp. 424–428.

Vassian Patrikeev. "Polemicheskija sochinenija vassiana patrikeev." *Prav. sob*, Tome III (1863), pp. 208ff.

C. Particular Bibliography Dealing with Nil Sorsky

Arxangel'skij, A. S. "*Nil Sorsky i Vassian Patrikeev, ix literaturnye trudi i idei v drevnej rusi istoriko literaturnyi ocherk*, Part I: *Prepodobnyi Nil Sorsky*." *PDP*, no. 25. St. Petersburg, 1882.

Borovkova-Maikova, M. S. "Velikij starec Nil, pustynnik Sorsky." *Russkij filogicheskij vestnik*, Vol. LXIV (1910), pp. 62–78.

———. "K literaturnoj dejatel'nosti Nila Sorskogo." *PDP*, no. 177. St. Petersburg, 1910.

Fennell, J. L. G., "The Attitude of the Josephians and Trans-Volga Elders to the Heresy of the Judaizers." *Slavonic and East European Review*, XXIX (1951); 486–509.

Gorskij, A. "Otnoshenija inokov kirillova-belozerskago i iosifova volokolamskago monastyrej v xvi veke." *Prib. k tvor.*, vol. X (1851), pp. 502ff.

A SELECTED BIBLIOGRAPHY

Kalestinov, K. *Velikij starec. ocherk zhizni prepodobnogo Nila Sorskogo.* St. Petersburg, 1907.

Kologrivov, I. *Essai sur la sainteté en russie,* pp. 187–213. Bruges, 1953.

Lilienfeld, Fairy von. "Josif Volockij und Nil Sorskij, ihre sogenannten 'schulen' und ihre stellung im gesellschafthlich und politischen leben ihrer zeit." *Zeitschr. f. S.,* no. 3 (1958), pp. 786–801.

Lure, S. J. "K voprosu ob ideologii Nila Sorskogo." *TODL,* vol. XVI (XIII (1957), pp. 182–212.

Nikol'skij, N. K. "O Vlijanii vizantijskix uchenij na Nila Sorskogo." *Visantijskij Vremennik* III (1895), pp. 192–195.

Pokrovskij, K. V. "K Literaturnoj dejatel'nosti Nila Sorskogo." Trudy Drevnosti, *Slavjanskoj komiissi mosk. arx. obshch.,* Vol. V, Protokol 103. Moscow, 1911.

Pravdin, A. "Prepodobnyj Nil Sorskij i ustave ego skitskoj zhizni." *Xristianskoje chtenie,* Jan. 1877, pp. 114–157.

Smolitsch, I., "Velikj starec Nil Sorskij." *PUT',* no. 19, Nov. 1919.

Uspenskij, F. *Ocherki po istorii vizantijskoj obrazavannosti.* St. Petersburg, 1892.

Index

References to material in the Introduction are in **boldface**.

Solitude, **20, 23,** 47, 108; *see also*
  Silence
Sorsky, Nil. *See* Nil Sorsky
Spiritual guides, **19,** 48
Strigol'niki, **11**
Suffering, 79–83, 128–35
Suggestion, 50–52
Symeon the Studite, **30,** 47
Symeon the New Theologian, St.,
  22, 29, 30, 47, 48; gift of
  tears, 98–99, 101; ineffable
  joy, 61; prayer, **12, 28,** 55, 56,
  64, 82, 101; silence, 108;
  suggestion, 50; weeping
  without tears, 102

Tears, gift of, **27,** 98–105;
  cultivation of, 104–5; prayer
  for, 98–99, 100–102; seeking,
  99–100; value of, 103–4
Temptations, **20,** 53, 65–66, 70–77,
  116–20; to pride, 87; *see also*
  Thoughts; Vices
Theodore the Studite, **30,** 89
Thoughts, psychology of, **20–21;**
  captivity or enslavement, 52;
  consenting to suggestions,
  51–52; cultivation of inner

attentiveness, 66–67;
  dialoguing, 50–51; emptying
  of, **24,** 54; evil thoughts, 52,
  53–58, 65–70, 118, 121–22;
  guarding the thought, 65;
  suggestion, 50–52; *see also*
  Passions; *Tradition* (Nil
  Sorsky). See *Predanie* (Nil
  Sorsky)
Trans-Volga hermits, **11, 33**
Trinity, **17, 21, 22**
Tushin, Gurii: Nil Sorsky's letter
  to, 121–25

Ustav (Nil Sorsky), **14–15, 25, 28,
  30, 31, 35;** text, 46–115

Vainglory, 63, 84–85; *see also* Pride
Vassian Patrikeev, Prince, 34: Nil
  Sorsky's letter to, 116–20
Velitchkovsky, Paisy, St., **35, 36**
Vices, **20,** 71–90
Vigilance, **25–26**
Vitaly, Justin, Bishop, **36–37**
Volokolamsk, Joseph. *See* Joseph of
  Volokolamsk

Women, 45